CONTENTS

i

KU-485-111

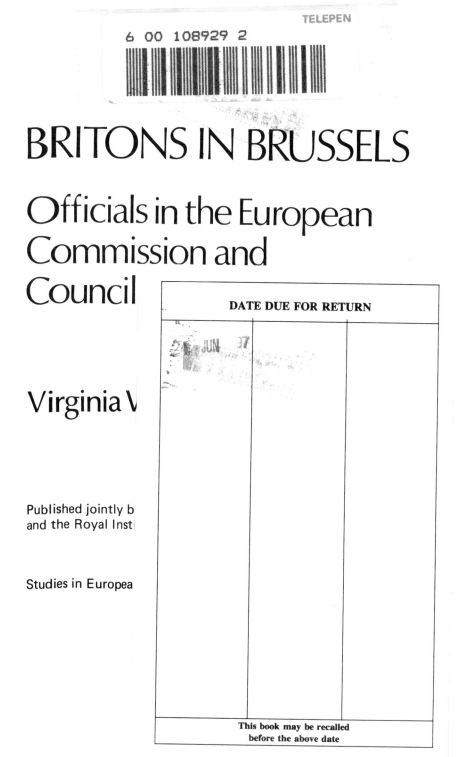

BRITONS IN BRUSSELS

Officials in the European Commission and Council

Virginia V

Published jointly b
and the Royal Inst

Studies in Europea

ISBN 0 85374-217-0

Published by Policy Studies Institute, 1–2 Castle Lane, London SW1E 5DR
Printed by Bourne Offset Ltd.

Preface

This study is concerned with an aspect of the European Community's institutions which has attracted a certain degree of public interest, namely the question of their staffing. Where do the 'Eurocrats' come from? If they come from the Civil Service of their own member states, do they transfer their loyalties to Brussels, or do they act as agents for their own country within the European bureaucracy - or perhaps some mixture of the two? How successful has the Community been in evolving an administrative ethos based on an amalgam of different national ones, and how does the European bureaucracy differ from, say, the Secretariat of the United Nations? The fact that this important range of questions had so far been very inadequately studied led to the planning and commissioning of the present research study as a joint enterprise of the European Centre for Political Studies at PSI and the Royal Institute of Public Administration.

The research carried out by Virginia Willis sheds light on these questions and others, by means of a detailed examination of the position and experience of British officials working for the Commission and the Council Secretariat of the Community. Although the study draws some general conclusions, it should be said that its main focus is that of an examination in depth of a specific part of the field. In the planning of the study, it was agreed that attention would be paid to two of the European Community's institutions - the Commission and the Council - rather than to others (for instance the European Parliament or the Economic and Social Committee); secondly, attention has deliberately been focused on the experience of one member state, the United Kingdom (although plans are being made to follow this pilot study by comparable enquiries concerning other countries); and thirdly, the main concern of the study is with the 'public administration' aspects of the subject, notably the process of recruitment of Eurocrats and their experience of working in Brussels. This concentration of focus means that other issues, for instance the political role of senior Eurocrats, or their sometimes negative public image, have not been covered in the study. These questions are of course related to the more specific enquiry which has been undertaken here, and they should be high on the agenda for future research in this field.

The present study thus reflects, in considerable detail, the experience and preoccupations of one member state: the United Kingdom. It does, however, raise questions of a fundamental kind about the staffing and functioning of the Community's key institutions as a whole, and its conclusions should be taken into account by all who are concerned to make these institutions work better in future.

Roger Morgan

Foreword

Even before the United Kingdom joined the European Community there was speculation about how British staff would be recruited to the Community institutions, and especially to the Commission. Questions were raised as to whether it would be permanent appointees from a variety of professional backgrounds or primarily civil servants on secondment who went to serve Europe from Britain, and what possible influence their experience in the Community might have in bringing change to British traditions of public administration.(1) Reflection on speculations of this kind stimulated this attempt to look at the contribution made in practice over the past ten years by the British to the staffing of the Commission and the General Secretariat of the Council of Ministers of the European Communities, to analyse the backgrounds of those who went to Brussels, to describe their experience there, and to relate it all to perspectives and procedures in Whitehall. If focusing in this way on one nationality, in the context of a Community 'where all are Europeans in the service of Europe' needs justification, it is that there is now concern about disparities in the comparative contributions to staffing by the member states, and it is in the European interest to try to identify their causes in order that they may be remedied.

It is intended that this account of Britons as officials in two Community institutions will be followed shortly by parallel studies of nationals from other member states employed there. Meanwhile it is hoped that this account will have an intrinsic interest for what it says about the experience of Britons in Brussels, and also for what it reflects of Whitehall and its relations with the Community in an area about which little information has so far been published. Material on which it is based comes from two main sources: firstly, interviews in Brussels with Community officials of all nationalities, with former Community officials in Brussels and London, and with serving or retired British civil servants in London; and secondly, material generously made available to me by Community authorities in Brussels and the Civil Service Department, as it then was, in London. The interviews on the experience of Britons in Brussels were conducted between autumn 1980 and autumn 1981, on the basis of a questionnaire with a random selection of 15 per cent of officials in the Commission and Council in each of the A grades. Details of the survey are given in Appendix I.

I am particularly grateful to the authorities in the Commission and the Council, and to the former Civil Service Department, for their co-operation in this study, as well as to all those interviewed, for their generosity with their time and attention, and for making the interviews so enjoyable as well as interesting and informative. I hope they will feel that a balanced, accurate and acceptable account is presented here of the experience of 'Britons in Brussels'.

Thanks are also due to those who commented so helpfully on the drafts, particularly Dr Helen Wallace and Dr Roger Morgan, to Amanda Trafford and Avis Lewallen of the European Centre for Political Studies at PSI, to the editor Mrs Margaret Cornell, and to my husband for his support and encouragement. Responsibility for any errors, omissions or infelicities is mine alone, and opinions expressed here are not the responsibility of any other person or of the institutes sponsoring the study.

NOTE
(1)   David Coombes, Towards a European Civil Service, Chatham House/PEP, European Series No.7, 1968, pp.59ff.

I STAFFING IN THE COMMISSION AND COUNCIL SECRETARIAT

The appropriate staffing of multinational organisations is notoriously liable to practical and diplomatic difficulties. The secretariats of all international organisations have found it hard to create a viable career structure with appropriate personnel resources. The Secretariat General of the United Nations presents perhaps the best known example of the problems of running a multinational administration, and in particular of the perennial concern to ensure an equitable geographical distribution of posts.(1)   It had been hoped to avoid such problems in the Commission of the European Community and the General Secretariat of the Council of Ministers. In practice, however, it has proved difficult to establish an independent and multinational European career civil service, such as early idealists had envisaged. Changing attitudes amongst member states to the ideal of European integration have changed the course on which the institutions were first set. They are encountering now some of the problems common to more orthodox international organisations, notably that of striking an acceptable balance of nationalities in different posts at all levels. Heightened interest in the nationality aspects of Community staffing may have been stimulated by successive reorganisations imposed by the merger of the executives of the European Coal and Steel Community, EURATOM, and the European Economic Community in 1967, and the enlargements in 1973 and 1981, when room had to be made for the officials of the new member states through the redisposition or retirement of some of those from the old. Concern has been voiced about disparities in national contributions to staffing by Members of the European Parliament in Strasbourg, and of the Parliaments of some member states, and by officials too, both in the Community institutions in Brussels and in some national administrations. Member state governments, while on the one hand inclined sometimes to prefer

1

lame-duck Community institutions on a narrow view of national interest, are generally concerned with a wider vision, to see that Community institutions are as effective and as efficient as possible. They are increasingly aware of the importance of a balance amongst the nationalities on the staff, and anxious to ensure that their countries make a suitable contribution to the staffing of those institutions, not merely in terms of numbers but also of quality, distribution, and effectiveness. It is against this background, in a context where all Community officials are first and foremost Europeans in the service of Europe, that the contributions of individual member states such as the UK should be discussed.

The General Secretariat of the Council of Ministers

The General Secretariat of the Council of Ministers performs tasks akin to those of other secretariats, such as NATO, OECD or GATT. The Council of Ministers, composed of the ministers of member states appropriate to the subject under discussion, is now the predominant decision-making body of the Commmunity, despite the early expectations of many of the founding fathers that this role would fall to the Commission. Its staff have the task of organising and administering the Council and preparing its decisions. They prepare briefs for the Council members, and particularly for the incumbent President, who changes every six months with the rotation of the Presidency between the member states. Briefs do not so much contain material for discussion in council as an outline of the progress of particular proposals, originating from the Commission, through the institutions, discussing what the potential problems or snags might be. The Council Secretariat must be seen to be independent of the member states in order to maintain their confidence. Staff are, for example, scrupulously careful to avoid becoming a tool for the national interests of the member state holding the Presidency.

The Commission

The Commission's role is quite different from that of a secretariat, and is unparalleled amongst international organisations. Its functions as the engine of integration are central to the Community. It is obliged by the Treaties to make proposals for new policies or changes in policy upon which the Council must decide, an obligation which is extremely important because, under the Treaties, the Council can take decisions only on the basis of proposals by the Commission, and any amendment to a Commission proposal has to be decided by unanimity. As well as generating positive new thinking, the Commission also has to act as a mediator, reconciling

2

the different interests, whether national, regional, sectoral or functional, and matching the expertise of its interlocutors on a wide range of technical areas. It administers common policies agreed by the Council, notably the Common Agricultural Policy, the Common Commercial Policy, the Regional and Social Policies. It also has a supervisory role, checking that Community regulations and directives are appropriately carried out by the governments of member states who are required to enact them. If necessary it can initiate action in the European Court of Justice against member states who do not carry out their obligations, monitoring the fulfilment of those obligations as part of its role as guardian of the Treaties upon which the Community is founded. As the 'conscience of Europe' it embodies 'the whole against the national parts', and puts the European perspective where the national viewpoints are articulated in the Council of Ministers.(2) Finally, the Commission also negotiates on behalf of the Community its external commercial relations, dealing with other international organisations or non-member states in accordance with mandates from the Council.

The principles of Community staffing
The way in which the Commission fulfills its functions is crucial to the way the European Community operates. The Commission's unique combination of administrative and political functions endows the subject of how and by whom it is staffed with a particular interest and importance. Given the sensitivity of member states to the areas of what used to be national policy which now fall wholly or partly within Community competence, it is essential that the Commission and its staff, together with that of the other institutions, should be seen to be neutral between them and independent of them.

This was recognised from the earliest days of the Communities. The Commissioners themselves are required by the Treaty of Rome to carry out their functions 'in complete independence' and 'in the general interest of the Community', 'neither requesting nor accepting instructions from any government or from any other body'.(3) The regulations governing the staff are no less strict. Dating from 1962 and designed to protect the independence of the institution, they insist that an official's first obligation is to do his job 'having solely in view the interests of the Communities, without soliciting or accepting instructions from any government authority or organisation or person extraneous to his institution'.(4)

Even so, the political implications of the early visions of a completely independent supranational body of Eurocrats encroach-

3

ing on national prerogatives proved unacceptable to the member states. The French, for example, have consistently argued for a Commission composed of seconded national civil servants, and like other member states they have made it their practice to send a significant number to the Commission. As a result of reservations of this kind amongst member states, the Commission has pragmatically evolved as an independent service which has at the same time accommodated the political dimension of staffing, by recognising the inevitable and legitimate interest of member state governments in appointments to the top levels of policy-making.(5)

Other qualities besides independence from outside influence are required of Commission officials. Under the regulations recruits are to possess 'the highest qualities of competence, performance, and integrity'(6). A key additional requirement in the early days was that staff should be devoted Europeans, who by their zeal and commitment to the goal of integration would maintain the momentum of the Commission's progress towards it. Though loyalty to the European ideal has remained important, more tangible qualities have increasingly been sought, especially since the dispute between France and her partners in 1965-6. The functions of the Commission demand a high degree of technical expertise from officials if they are to be able to deal on equal terms with political and professional groups in all the different member states, as well as political sensitivity and a detailed knowledge of the policies and legislation of the member states. All these qualities are needed in an organisation which is tiny in comparison with national administrations, and which has to work in several languages.

Distribution of nationalities
Commission staff regulations also require that officials be recruited 'on the widest possible geographical basis amongst the nationals of member states'.(7) Any suggestion of formal national quotas would be rejected out of hand as totally contrary to the spirit of Europeanism on which the Community is based, and as impinging on the vital independence of the Commission, restricting its ability to select the best possible candidates to serve regardless of nationality. Nevertheless, the need to keep a balance amongst nationalities on the staff has always been recognised as important. At the inception of the EEC, when idealism about European integration was high, there was a gentlemen's agreement that posts should be divided between the six member states in proportion to each country's contribution to the Community budget.(8) With the decline of that idealism, an adequate national balance remains one key to maintaining both the actual and the perceived independence

4

of the Commission, and to retaining member states' confidence in the truly European nature of the institution. It is a principle which constitutes at one level a means of neutralising any possible untoward national influences which would undermine the effectiveness of the Commission, and at another an important facet of its day-to-day working.

Importance to Commission

The Commission itself seeks to maintain a geographical balance amongst officials 'not so much to ensure equilibrium at a given moment by earmarking posts by nationality, but to benefit in a positive dynamic way from the varied experience which officials of different nationalities can bring, and to achieve a balance over a period of time'.(9) It has a particular need to take account in its proposals and activities of national attitudes, policies, procedures, and personalities, which nationals of each country are most likely to know and understand thoroughly. It specifically needs the expertise in legal, financial and political systems which they can bring. Their specialised understanding of national considerations is essential in making sure that important national preoccupations are not overlooked at the policy-making stages and in the negotiating and implementing stages which follow. Member state nationals on the staff are an essential part of the two-way network of information, ideas and contacts between the national authorities and the Commission, crucial to the formulation and enforcement of valid and workable policies. In short, an adequate geographical balance amongst Community officials contributes to an adequate institutional understanding of each member state and a mutual confidence which facilitates the progress of Commission business.

The member states who joined the Community at successive enlargements, and especially the United Kingdom, the largest of them, have a particular contribution to make in the area of 'institutional understanding'. The Anglo-Saxon legal and administrative traditions, for example, are different from those of the UK's Community partners, and the Community institutions, set up before she became a member, need now to encompass something of these traditions to have the full confidence of all member states. There is a lot of leeway to make up, to convert institutions whose administrations are historically weighted in favour of the traditions of the old Community of the Six to adequate representation of the differing traditions of the Ten. If they fail to make the maximum possible contribution, the new member states are failing to ensure adequate institutional understanding of their systems and thinking, and so contributing to the undermining of the Community's ability to be fully catholic and therefore effective.

5

Less than adequate national representation amongst Community officials, especially in areas where the Community has strong powers, as in Competition and Agriculture, can breed a certain inhibition to full co-operation amongst national officials with whom they have contact. If national officials feel that they are dealing in the Commission almost exclusively with 'foreigners' who have actual or potential authority over policy sectors of importance to them but no deep understanding of the special factors applying in their particular country, mistrust and a reluctance to co-operate fully can result. National officials can become distanced from the Commission and approach issues with increasingly negative instructions, reluctant above all to transfer competence to institutions where they find insufficient understanding. This has reportedly been the experience of the Dutch, who feel that their under-representation has been one factor in a waning enthusiasm for the Community perceived amongst officials in Home Departments in The Hague. As one official said of the situation, 'not respecting this nationality question was a luxury allowed only in the past'. Mutual trust and understanding tend to flow more easily between officials with a common national background and the efficient working of the Commission depends on such trust.

Importance to member states

A recent review of the workings of the Commission undertaken in 1979 by an independent group under the chairmanship of Mr Dirk Spierenburg reported: 'It is in everyone's self-interest that the Commission should perform its many tasks efficiently and effectively'.(10) The Community and the national interests are indivisible on this issue of geographical representation, as in others. Just as the Commission needs national expertise in the making of Community policy, so member states are understandably concerned to see that their nationals, fully aware of the national circumstances in any given policy area, are participating in the making of that policy. This is especially so if the policy areas are of particular relevance to vital national interests. Community decisions after all have a direct influence on social and economic conditions in each member country. This is recognised explicitly at the topmost level, and each member state has at least one Commissioner, with the 'big four', Italy, France, Germany and the UK, having two each. Though the Commissioners are nominated by the member state governments and confirmed by the Council of Ministers, their independence should be beyond doubt. Below them there is a rudimentary system of checks and balances to try to eliminate any overwhelming influence by any one nation in any one

6

policy area. Commissioners do not normally have top officials, Directors General, of the same nationality administering the areas for which they are responsible, and there is an attempt to distribute the top three grades within a department or directorate-general among as many nationalities as possible. At the top level - and to a decreasing extent at the next level - governments have a substantial say in the choice of candidates for appointment. They sometimes 'parachute' candidates from outside in to top jobs, as well as bringing influence to bear in the filling of vacancies from 'inside the house', which is strongly affected by considerations of 'geographical balance'. There is inevitably a certain amount of horse-trading over these appointments between member state governments, and though the final decision lies with the College of Commissioners, which will in principle prefer the best qualified candidate for the job, nationality can be an important consideration.

Even below these top policy-making levels, however, member state governments increasingly perceive it as important to have as many competent nationals on the staff as possible. As one commentator has remarked, 'It is generally agreed that France's interests were well served as a result of its policy of sending highly competent officials to fill senior positions in the Commission, while Germany's interests were less competently represented when the Federal Republic made the mistake (subsequently rectified) of being less selective'.(11) Ability has always been important but is now at an increased premium because promotion to all grades, including the topmost, is made increasingly from within the institutions, as the Commission works to improve the career prospects of its officials by reducing apppointments from outside. Already 70 per cent of officials in the two top grades have been promoted into them. The middle and lower grades thus constitute the seed corn for the top appointments and are the key to an appropriate geographical balance in the future. Without a blend of quality and adequate national balance at this level, it will be increasingly difficult to fill top posts adequately. The newer member governments have been somewhat slow to appreciate this point, however.

Pledged as they are to eschew national bias, and despite their high concept of service to the Community ideal, Community officials find it virtually impossible and even undesirable to liquidate all national consciousness or national characteristics. This has important practical implications even at the middle and lower levels of policy-making.

Commission proposals are the starting point of legislation, whether regulations which enter directly into national law or directives and decisions, which, for example, in setting harmonised standards in areas as diverse as car exhausts, mercury thermometers, abattoirs and turkey plucking, can have enormous implications for the industries affected by them. Drafting officials try to collect details of practices and preferences in each member state before preparing their draft proposals. The Commission has extensive recourse to meetings of national experts for this purpose. Nevertheless, individual officials will tend to have the best understanding of their own national experience and to find it easiest to deal with their own nationals, so that it would not be surprising if draft proposals had an unconscious bias to the advantage of the officials' own member states. One observer claims that national influence in drafting can be more direct, and that the French in particular have a reputation for getting nationals to introduce papers drafted in the national capital as their own work.(12) Any unintentional national bias will probably be ironed out in the progress of the draft through the Community's processes. However, specific problems for member states or national industries may be caused on the way with points of interest lost or traded in the negotiating process, involving considerable effort to correct any such bias.

Similarly, experience and perceptions reflecting national background and culture can affect the way in which specifications for contracts and programmes for Community funding are drawn up. There is competition for Community funds under such programmes as the Social Fund and the Regional Development Fund. The presence in a division or directorate-general of a large contingent of óne nationality may be interpreted as producing a certain bias in the criteria for the disbursement of funds or contracts, especially those where the Commission officials can exercise discretion. The House of Lords Select Committee on Development Aid policy in the EEC(13) found that of the lucrative contracts given out under the Lome Conventions, Britain received only 11 per cent compared with 33 per cent won by the French. It suggested that one reason for this was that the key posts in the upper echelons of the administration in Brussels were staffed predominantly by French nationals, and went on to urge the British Government to 'insert' more officials into the relevant department.

There is the additional point that information is usually more freely exchanged informally between compatriots, who provide likely first access points for outsiders faced with the apparently baffling monolith of the Berlaymont. It is useful not only to government officials, but also to interested parties from industry, commerce and local government who are likely to be affected, to be party to some of the thinking going into a decision or proposal, just as it is useful for Commission officials to have their views. The 'quiet word' which may be effective at an early stage before hard negotiations begin is more easily exchanged with and perhaps more readily understood by fellow countrymen. Especially in the Commission, which is deliberately permeable and more open to access than most national administrations, it is advantageous for a member state to have a maximum number of its nationals in areas of greatest interest to it, so that government officials or representatives of industry can pick up early warning of likely developments and even influence them through lobbying. Less than the maximum number of access points can render more difficult the work of such representatives, whether from government or industry. Such considerations underline how important it is both to member states and to the Community itself that the 'geographic balance' is maintained more or less in equilibrium throughout the Community institutions, but especially at the policy-making levels in the Commission.

Organisation of staff
The organisation of staff within the two institutions with which we are chiefly concerned, the Commission and the General Secretariat of the Council of Ministers, has particular features which need to be identified before we can look at how geographical balance applies in practice.

Both are divided into a number of administrative units. In the Commission (in 1980) 13 Commissioners, each of whom has a personal office or cabinet of as many as 15 members (with some five or six A-grade officials some of whom are often seconded for a limited period from their national administrations or political parties) divide between them responsibility for some 29 administrative units dealing with the subjects assigned to them in their portfolios. Nineteen of the units are Directorates-General, dealing with specific subjects and generally known by their numbers (for example DG I External Relations), and the others, besides the important and powerful Secretariat General, are functional and comprise the Legal Service, Publications Office, Statistics, Customs Union and the Environmental and Consumer Protection Unit. The biggest is DG VI, Agriculture, with some 640 staff in 1979, but they average about 230 staff. Each Directorate-General is headed by a Director-General, ranked A1, who in the larger units is supported by one or more deputy directors-general, also A1 (a titre personnel), and by several Directors or Principal Advisers at A2. Each Directorate is made up of several Divisions, headed by a Chef de Division of rank A3, or Specialised Services headed by an A4-5 official (a Principal Administrator). The rest of the A grades comprise A6-7 (Administrators), and a very few Assistant Administrators, A8. The A grades are the policy-makers, roughly comparable to the former Administrative grade in the UK Civil Service, and they comprise (see Table 1.1) about a quarter of the almost 9,000 non-research staff employed by the Commission, principally in Brussels and Luxembourg. They are complemented by language specialists, LA grade, who do translation and interpretation work, and supported by the largely non-graduate B category staff, comprising the executive officers and senior secretaries who form the backbone of most bureaucracies, the clerical and secretarial C grades and the D grade of drivers, messengers and skilled workers.

The requirements of a secretariat servicing the Council of Ministers dictate a different shaped structure with a larger proportion of language specialists and secretarial and clerical staff. The 1,500 staff are organised in a similar fashion to the Commission with two general departments, the Secretariat General and the Legal Department, and six Directorates-General, labelled A to F, dividing between them subjects such as agriculture, social policy, energy, etc.

Table 1.1   Council Secretariat and Commission of EEC: distribution of permanent staff by grade, 1980.

	A %	B %	C %	D %	LA %
Commission	26	22	34	5	13
Council Secretariat	12	9	48	13	18

(Taken from Commission and Council Sources: to nearest full percentage).

National balance in practice
From the earliest days care was taken to try to distribute posts in the Commission equally between member states. As we have seen,

10

posts were originally distributed by gentlemen's agreement in proportion to each country's contribution to the Community budget, but considerations of population and gross national product have come to be taken into account. In the Europe of the Six, the French, Germans and Italians were each expected to field about 25 per cent of the staff, and the Benelux nations the other 25 per cent between them. In fact, the proportions were only achieved in the topmost grades, and only roughly in the administrative cadre as a whole.(14)

At the first enlargement in 1973 it was expected that the larger countries, the UK, France, Germany and Italy, would each field 18.4 per cent of the total Commission staff, as would the Benelux countries together, with Ireland and Denmark contributing 4 per cent each. It was assumed that the other Community institutions would aim at a similar distribution. In fact, a precise equilibrium, like that projected for the Six, has never been reached. By the end of December 1974, the first year for which full figures are available, the Commission (see Table 1.2) calculated that there were only 8.4 per cent Britons in Commission service, compared with 16.3 per cent Germans, 14.9 per cent French, 16.7 per cent Italians, 37.3 per cent Beneluxers (comprising 26.2 per cent Belgians, 6 per cent Dutch and 5.1 per cent Luxemburgers), 3.7 per cent Danes and 1.9 per cent Irish. The proportion of British in other Community institutions was also under par, with 10 per cent on the staff of the Council Secretariat, 14.3 per cent at the Court of Justice, 11.9 per cent at the European Investment Bank, and 8.1 per cent in the Economic and Social Committee.(15) This was not perhaps surprising so soon after the UK had joined the Community. However, these proportions have not changed for the better. Indeed in 1977 Britons were quoted as forming an average of only 7 per cent of the staff of the Commission, the Council, the Parliament, the Court of Justice and the Economic and Social Committee.(16) The figures, for June and November 1980, for the Commission and Council show the proportions there to be 9.4 per cent and 7.9 per cent respectively. (See Appendix III and IV).

The greatest imbalances in both institutions are at the support staff levels. As the figures in Table 1.3 show, there is an overwhelming Belgian presence in the B and C grades in the Commission. The D grade has been traditionally dominated by Italians, who in 1980 made up 43.5 per cent of the messengers and drivers in the Commission, and nearly 50 per cent in the Council. At the C grade in the Commission, the 40 per cent Belgian contingent contrasted with the 15 per cent Italian, 11 per cent

11

German and French, 5 per cent UK, and among the smaller member states more comparable in size, the Danish 3 per cent, the Irish 2.1 per cent and the Dutch 3.4 per cent. The disparities in the Council are of the same order, where 25 per cent Belgians in the C grades contrast with 7 per cent Britons, and an average of 16 per cent amongst the larger nations. One effect of the disparities in this grade is that, even including the Irish, there is a desperate shortage of secretaries who have English as a first language, which could affect the performance of English-speaking members of the A grades. At the B grade in the Commission there is a similarly high proportion of Belgians - 28 per cent compared with 8.4 per cent from the UK, 16 per cent from Germany, 16.5 per cent from France, 13.5 per cent from Italy, 7.7 per cent from the Nether-lands, 2.5 per cent from Denmark and 1.2 per cent from Ireland. In the Council there were two Britons, one Irishman and no Danes, compared with 44 Belgians, 18 Germans, 23 Frenchmen and 14 Italians. It is an imbalance worrying to the personnel authorities in both institutions, who find that amongst candidates for vacancies at support staff level, the Belgians consistently present the highest number of suitable people. Proximity and familiarity with the institutions and their requirements must play a large part in this, but such an imbalance does have implications for the character of the institutions.

Though the B grades attract increasing interest, with repeated proposals that they should be promoted into the A levels in greater numbers, it is the policy-making A grades which command chief attention from member states. Here it is striking that while the proportion of staff from the largest original member states approx-imates to or exceeds proposed levels, the new member states and the Netherlands are under-represented. The Dutch view is that by the criteria of population, GNP and contribution to the Community budget, they should have between 9 and 10 per cent of posts. Their figure of 6 per cent in the A grades therefore causes them some concern.

Denmark and Ireland have 3 per cent of officials where they were expected to have 4 per cent, but it is the degree of the UK's under-representation that is most striking. There are even fewer British A grade officials per head than Dutch, and the proportion of 14 per cent British is both significantly below the 18.4 per cent projected in 1972 and the proportion from comparable member states. Whilst Belgium is hardly comparable to the UK by the three criteria, there are 13.3 per cent Belgians in the A grade. Moreover between 1974 and 1980, the proportion of Britons

12

Table 1.2   Permanent and temporary officials in the Commission, by nationality, 31 December 1974

Grade	UK No.	%	France No.	%	Germany No.	%	Italy No.	%	Belgium No.	%
A	296	14.9	369	18.5	373	18.7	363	18.2	261	13.1
B	100	7.3	235	17.2	270	19.7	191	14.0	318	23.2
C	87	3.3	338	12.9	356	13.6	363	13.8	1,044	39.8
D	6	1.7	23	6.6	19	5.5	148	42.7	120	34.6
LA	106	12.9	92	11.8	142	18.3	121	15.6	118	15.2
Total	595	8.4	1,057	14.9	1,160	16.3	1,861	16.7	1,861	26.2

Grade	Netherlands No.	%	Luxemburg No.	%	Denmark No.	%	Ireland No.	%	Others No.	Total
A	125	6.3	61	3.1	75	3.8	59	3.0	9	1,991
B	104	7.6	79	5.8	39	2.9	21	1.5	11	1,368
C	107	4.1	187	7.1	66	2.5	49	1.9	24	2,621
D	4	1.2	25	7.2	-	-	-	-	2	347
LA	85	10.9	10	1.3	82	10.5	6	0.8	16	778
Total	425	6.0	362	5.1	262	3.7	135	1.9	62	7,105

From Commission figures: see Appendix II.

13

Table 1.3 Commission officials by grade and nationality: 30 June 1980

Grade	UK No.	%	France No.	%	Germany No.	%	Italy No.	%	Belgium No.	%
A	325	14.3	462	20.4	427	18.8	396	17.5	301	13.3
B	156	8.4	305	16.5	300	16.2	249	13.5	515	27.8
C	145	4.9	333	11.2	326	11.0	444	15.0	1,181	39.9
D	10	2.4	18	4.3	16	3.8	179	43.5	147	35.7
LA	171	15.4	108	9.7	185	16.6	191	17.2	161	14.5
Total	807	9.4	1,226	14	1,254	14.6	1,459	17.0	2,305	26.8

Grade	Netherlands No.	%	Luxemburg No.	%	Denmark No.	%	Ireland No.	%	Others No.	Total
A	136	6.0	64	2.8	69	3.0	69	3.0	11	2,260
R	143	7.7	98	5.3	47	2.5	23	1.2	12	1,848
C	100	3.4	245	8.2	95	3.2	61	2.1	24	2,954
D	5	1.2	34	8.2	1	-	-	-	1	411
LA	108	9.7	10	1.0	112	10	13	1.2	49	1,108
Total	492	5.7	451	5.2	324	3.8	116	1.9	97	8,581

Source: Commission figures: see Appendix III.

14

Table 1.4   Commission officials by nationality in the 'A' grades: 30 June 1980

Grade	UK No.	%	France No.	%	Germany No.	%	Italy No.	%	Belgium No.	%
A1	7	16.6	8	19.0	8	19.0	7	16.6	5	11.9
A2	22	16.3	28	20.8	24	17.8	24	17.8	11	8.1
A3	52	16.3	57	17.9	60	18.8	55	17.2	35	10.9
A4	78	13.0	117	19.5	137	22.9	90	15.0	102	17.0
A5	72	14.6	92	18.7	85	17.3	109	22.2	57	11.6
A6	48	12.3	86	22.1	69	17.7	77	19.7	57	14.6
A7	46	16.3	74	26.2	44	15.6	34	12.1	34*	12.1
Total	325	14.4	462	20.4	427	18.9	396	17.5	301	13.3

Grade	Netherlands No.	%	Luxemburg No.	%	Denmark No.	%	Ireland No.	%	Others No.	Total
A1	3	7.1	1	2.4	2	4.8	1	2.4		42
A2	11	8.1	6	4.4	5	3.7	4	3.0		135
A3	26	8.1	10	3.1	11	3.4	12	3.8	2	320
A4	40	6.7	19	3.2	4	0.7	11	1.8	1	599
A5	27	5.5	14	2.8	18	3.7	17	3.5	1	492
A6	13	3.3	8	2.1	18	4.6	11	2.8	3	390
A7	16	5.7	6	2.1	11	3.9	13	4.6	4	287
Total	136	6.0	64	2.8	69	3.1	69	3.1	11	2.260

Source: As for Table 1.3
* Includes 1 at A/8.

Table 1.5 Member States of the European Community in relation to each other: 1980

Selected figures on the Community of Nine (in 1980)

Country	Popu- lation	GDP	Contribution to the budget Original own resources	Contribution to the budget VAT	Contribution to the budget Total	Category A# staff at the Commission on 1 January 1980 %
Belgium	3.8	4.4	7.56	4.54	6.17	13.5
Denmark	2.0	2.5	2.16	2.62	2.38	3.0
FR of Germany	23.5	30.5	27.26	32.80	29.81	19.0
France	20.6	24.1	14.09	24.67	18.96	20.2
Ireland	1.3	0.6	0.93	0.86	0.90	2.9
Italy	21.9	14.0	12.76	10.90	11.90	17.4
Luxembourg	0.1	0.2	0.05	0.20	0.12	2.9
Netherlands	5.4	6.0	10.92	6.05	8.68	6.0
United Kingdom	21.4	17.8	24.27	17.36	21.08	14.5
Total	100	100	100	100	100	99.4

Adapted from a table in Daniel Strasser, The Finances of Europe, European Perspectives: Commission of the EEC, Brussels, 1981, p.345. (Percentages of A grade officials differ slightly from those quoted elsewhere in this chapter because they are based on figures collected at a different time.

actually declined from 14.9 to 14.4 per cent, while amongst comparable states, the German proportion increased from 18.7 to 18.9 per cent and the French from 18.5 to 20.4 per cent. In numerical terms, the UK had in 1980 91 fewer nationals than she might have done helping to make Community policy in the Commission, and in the Council she was some 5, or 15 per cent, under par.

Distribution of Britons

Numbers are the main criterion used to consider 'geographical balance', but distribution of nationalities between jobs of perceived importance is also a factor. In accord with the ideal of a truly 'European' Civil Service, no breakdowns of the nationalities within Directorates-General are published. It is possible, however, to put together an approximate profile of the British presence. At the top level of Director-General, the five nationality groups, the UK, France, Germany, Italy and Benelux filled four posts each after enlargement, with one Irish Director-General and two Danish. At this level the distribution is rarely out of balance. Director-General posts are assigned with some regard to the interests which governments have in the subject of the Directorate-General, bearing in mind that Directors-General should not usually be of the same nationality as their Commissioners, and that posts are not supposed to be reserved for one particular nationality. Thus a Frenchman is Director-General of Agriculture and a German heads the Competition Directorate. Even at A1 level not all the posts are of major interest, and there is an equitable division of these posts too. In 1973 when Britain's first Commissioners, Sir Christopher Soames and George Thomson, held portfolios respectively for External Affairs and Regional Policy, British nationals held Director-Generalships in the Industrial Affairs, Social Affairs, Transport, and Scientific and Technical Information Directorates-General. After the change of Commissioners and portfolios in 1977 Roy Jenkins became President of the Commission with the Legal Service, Secretariat General, Spokesman's Group and Information, and Security Office portfolios, and Christopher Tugendhat took on the Budget, Financial Institutions and Personnel and Administration. It then became possible for UK nationals to head the External Affairs Directorate and the Energy Directorate-General in exchange for Industrial Affairs and Social Affairs respectively. The range of A1 posts held by Britons was appropriate for an energy-rich nation dependent on external trade, with an interest in these areas and experience and expertise to offer.

17

At the A2 Director and Chief Adviser level, the UK, with her special and different legal and administrative traditions, included in her complement two Britons among the seven senior men in the Commission's Secretariat General and two out of eleven in the Legal Service, and again made a fitting contribution. At this level too, a strong British presence in DG II, Economic and Financial Affairs, in DG IV the Competition Directorate-General, in the Department of the Budget DG XIX and in the Information Director-ate-General DG X seemed appropriate, though, in terms of numbers, in 1980 the UK had only 22 A2 posts compared with an average for France, Germany and Italy of 25. When the A3 posts are taken into account (and in 1980 the UK, with 52 posts, was five posts down on the average of the other large member states), some surprising lacunae appear in her presence in the top levels as a whole. In 1980 there was no Briton at A1-A3 in the Fisheries Directorate-General, DG XIV, an area where the UK's point of view was substantially different from that of her partners, nor in DG XVI, dealing with Regional Policy, where the UK has a special concern, nor (though she is over-represented in the rest of the DG) in the division dealing with the Social Fund in DG V, Social Affairs, which disburses funds of interest and importance to the UK.

Table 1.6   Numbers of British 'A' grades in the Commission compared with the average of those from comparable states. June 1980

	A1	A2	A3	A4-5	A6-7
UK	7	22	52	150	94
Average	7.7	25	57	210	128

Source: As for Table 1.3.

Taking all the A grades together, the UK had her strongest presence in the Information Directorate-General (an estimated 23 per cent); in the Directorate-General of the Budget, where in 1980 she fielded a Commissioner, an A2, an A3 and an estimated 21 per cent of all A grades; and in the Economic and Financial Affairs Directorate-General, where her financial expertise and City inter-ests are probably reflected by her estimated 21 per cent represen-tation. There were some 18 per cent Britons in DG VII, Transport, where there was a British Director-General, and 16 per cent in DG

18

VIII, Development. In some areas of particular relevance such as Energy (about 12 per cent) and External Affairs (about 15 per cent) she was under-represented, but sheer numbers were complemented by the presence of a Briton as Director-General. In areas where funds were disbursed, Britons seemed substantially under-represented, with only 10.5 per cent in DG VI, Agriculture, 9 per cent in DG XVI, Regional Policy, and 12.3 per cent in DG V, Social Affairs. Though it would be impractical to expect a consistent level of national representation in each DG, an inadequate presence in important areas is the likely corollary of insufficient numbers.

Prospects for change

The situation is all the more serious because it is difficult to amend without a radical change on which it would be difficult to win agreement. At the first enlargement there was only a limited period during which there were special arrangements for the recruitment of new member state nationals at all levels. Though there is the special dispensation for 'parachuting' recruits from outside the Commission into A1 and decreasingly A2 jobs where appropriate vacancies and candidates can be matched, such appointments are, as we have seen, increasingly being made by promotions from inside the house. While it has in the past been possible to appoint A2, A3 or even A4-5 officials by the somewhat devious means of a candidate being appointed on a temporary contract and subsequently established as a full official by means of an internal competition at which his special experience ensured his success, this device has been largely extinguished, and was anyway not very much used by the new member states. Since the implementation of one of the recommendations of the Spierenburg Report only 20 per cent of the A3 appointments made in any one year may go to outsiders. Virtually the only way into A4-5 is now by recruitment at the lowest level A6-7, through the infrequent open competitions, and a long wait for promotion. This battening down of the hatches has had the effect of focusing the attention of member states on the levels below the A1-3 grades which had previously been of prime interest. What they have seen has caused some of them concern because of the implications for their future representation in the topmost grades. In 1980 there were 150 Britons in the A4-5 grades (from which most future A3s would need to come), compared with 220 Germans, 209 French, 199 Italians and even 159 Belgians, while the Irish and the Danes, with 28 and 22 respectively, were also at a disadvantage.

While nationality factors are important in the senior grades, ability is more so and there is therefore a particular premium on

19

the potential for promotion of those in the A4-5 grades. The consensus amongst concerned observers is that, while the British include those of top quality among their number at every grade, there is a particular weakness at A4-5, 'a mixed bag', which does not encourage confidence that all the gaps at A3 and above can be easily filled. At the entry level A6-7, British candidates do not do badly, with roughly as many passing the examination as from other large member states, and a take-up rate of jobs second only to that of France. The success rate of UK candidates, like that of the other deficit nations, needs, however, to outstrip by far that of the other countries in order merely to make up the deficit at A6 and to approach par in A6-7 as a whole.

Aware of the need to take steps to equalise national balances, and under pressure from the under-represented member states, the Commission decided to give a special emphasis to the recruitment of candidates from the under-represented nations in exploiting the reserve lists established by the 1982 competition. The success of this initiative remains to be seen, but it is clear that there is room for a whole range of measures to be taken to equalise the balance, both by the Community authorities and concerned member states.

Possible causes of shortfalls

First, however, the root causes of under-representation need to be identified. There are different aspects to the problem in the different member states. The current Dutch difficulty arises from the fact that, although a good team of officials in terms of numbers and quality was sent to the top-level jobs in Brussels in the early days of membership, insufficient attention was paid then by the national authorities to the age structure in the senior positions, or to the filling and monitoring of the junior and middle-range posts, from which vacancies at a senior level have had increasingly to be filled. Thus when a number of Dutch Directors retired within a short space of time, it proved less than easy to find suitable candidates for promotion to re-establish the balance. At the same time, at the entry levels Dutch candidates were not doing sufficiently well in the entrance examinations, reflecting the differences between the training given to Dutch students and the requirements of the entry tests. 'There is room', reported a Dutch enquiry, 'for some scepticism concerning the chances of Dutch candidates getting through the competition'.(17) Concern at the Dutch situation was expressed in several discussions in the national Parliament, and when he was Vice-President of the European Parliament, Mr Vredeling took the initiative in the autumn of 1979 in launching an enquiry into why there were so few Dutch in the

Commission. In The Hague, the interdepartmental Management Committee for International Civil Servants actively sought ways of promoting the secondment of Dutch officials to the Community by improving the conditions governing their special leave of absence and publicising widely any vacancies, and more specifically organising workshops and seminars with mock competitions before open competitions for the A grade.

The problems are slightly different for the new member states, though officials from all four nations with significant under-representation remark on the lack of information about the Community and employment opportunities there at all levels. There is evidence that in the Commission, where there is a very low turnover of staff, the new member state nationals have a rate of resignation or requests to leave on personal grounds which is above average. The Danes are said to have a high turnover at the top levels. They tend to find the size and the formal hierarchical structure particularly foreign to their more youthful, direct and informal style of administration at home, while the high salaries in Denmark render Commission salaries small incentive to stay in Brussels. The highly developed pattern of two-career marriages in Denmark also makes it particularly difficult for families to move to Brussels without one spouse's career being disrupted. At the entry levels too the Community generally has not been popular with the young professionals who are potential candidates, and there is a certain Scandinavian unfamiliarity with the prevailing French language and cultural atmosphere in the Community which acts as a further deterrent. This last has been a factor with the Irish too, compounded by the distance of Brussels from Ireland and a general lack of familiarity with the institutions, especially in the early years of membership. The combination of ignorance and distance, as an Irish official commented, is unbeatable as a deterrent to good candidates. Amongst national officials, a likely source of recruits, the Commission has in the past had a low reputation, and this, combined with the lack of any return ticket scheme for officials willing to take a chance, or any possibility of promotion in absentia, did not render applications to the Commission very plentiful in 1972. Until quite recently, Irish administrators in Dublin remained somewhat blind to the implications of the nationality factor in Community staffing, their awakening interest being accelerated when the Irish Commissioner received the portfolio for Personnel in the Commission in 1981.

In a debate on 31 May 1977(18) in the European Parliament at Strasbourg on the Commission's recruitment policy, initiated by a

21

Table 1.7 Resignations from the Commission staff: British (others)

	1976		1977		1978		1979		Summer 1980	
A1	-	(-)	1	(-)	-	(-)	-	(-)	-	(-)
A2	-	(1)	2	(-)	2	(-)	1	(1)	-	(1)
A3	-	(2)	2	(1)	1	(1)	1	(1)	2	(-)
A4/8	1	(2)	4	(6)	-	(6)	3	(9)	4	(4)
B	1	(5)	2	(7)	1	(11)	2	(9)	2	(6)
C	2	(36)	4	(22)	3	(30)	8	(28)	2	(5)
D	-	(-)	-	(-)	-	(1)	1	(1)	-	(-)
LA	-	(6)	5	(8)	-	(6)	2	(6)	1	(3)
Total	4	(52)	20	(44)	7	(56)	18	(55)	11	(19)

Source: EEC Commission, IX.A.4, April 1980.

concerned British MEP, some reasons for the under-representation of the newer member states were discussed. The failure of the special recruiting operation for nationals of those new member states at the first enlargement in 1973 to attract enough people was cited as a major cause, and undoubtedly, as was suggested, 'some of the lack of success in those attempts came from the unwillingness of the horse to drink the water when it was offered'. Contributory factors included the cultural and geographical distance from home, and a tradition in Britain and Ireland of emigration to the English-speaking nations rather than to the Continent. In the case of the UK early doubts as to the strength of Britain's commitment to Community membership may also have played a part. The Commissioner for Personnel, Mr Tugendhat, who happened to be British, suggested as a further reason the high rate of resignations amongst Britons, a rate which is confirmed by the figures (see Table 1.7), though the actual numbers involved are not high and are comparable to those of the early resignations from the Commission by member state nationals of the Six(19), notably the Italians in 1961 and 1962. He suggested that the resignations were caused by 'linguistic and social factors' - the problems of living in a foreign culture and the effect on wives and families. On recruitment Mr Tugendhat suggested that there was 'a particularly

British problem'. 'Where you have a people who are less willing to move to the Continent than other people, where you have a particular country whose nationals unhappily tend to be less good at foreign languages and less willing to learn them than people from other countries, that country is always going to be at a disadvantage.'(20)

While such an analysis may be correct as far as it goes, it does not tell the whole story, as the following account of the experience of Britons who came to the Commission and Council suggests. However, there is no doubt that the special recruitment exercise of 1972-3 was crucial in determining the shape and quality of the British contribution to the staffing of Community institutions. It is therefore worth tracing the exercise and its difficulties in some detail.

NOTES

(1) S.D. Bailey, The Secretariat of the United Nations, UN Study, No.11, New York, 1962. Everyone's United Nations, 9th Edition, UN Publication, 1979, p.344.
(2) Stanley Henig, Power and Decision in Europe, Europotentials Press Ltd, 1980, p.39.
(3) Treaty establishing the EEC, Article 157.
(4) Statuts des fonctionnaires et le regime applicable aux autres agents de la CEE et de la CEEA, Article II, Journal Officiel des Communautes Europeennes, No.45, 1962, pp. 1383-1460.
(5) See E. Noel, 'The Committee of Permanent Representatives', Journal of Common Market Studies, Vol.V, 1967, No.3, pp.219-51.
(6) Statuts des fonctionnaires, op. cit, Art. XXVII.
(7) ibid.
(8) David Coombes, Politics and Bureaucracy in the EEC, Allen & Unwin, 1970, p.141.
(9) Proposals for Reform of the Commission of the European Communities and its Services. Report by an Independent Review Body under the Chairmanship of Mr Dirk Spierenburg, EEC Publication, 1979, p.22.
(10) ibid. p.3.
(11) Hans G. Michelmann, 'Multinational staffing and organisational functioning in the Commission of the EEC', International Organisation, Spring 1978, Vol.32, No.2. p.486.
(12) ibid.
(13) House of Lords, Select Committee Report on Development Aid Policy in the EEC, HL 80-81, 146 SS60, Rec.VII, p.XLIV.

(14) Daniel Strasser, The Finances of Europe, European Perspectives: EEC Commission, Brussels 1981, p. 316, quotes Germany 20 per cent (25 per cent A grade), France 17 per cent (A 23 per cent), Italy 18 per cent (A 21 per cent), Benelux 41 per cent (A 30 per cent).

(15) H.C. Debates, Vol.890 col.186 w, 18 April, 1975.

(16) European Parliament, Document 135/77, 31 May 1977, reported in Journal Officiel des Communautes Europeennes, No. 218, June 1977.

(17) Report from the Working Party on Workshops for potential candidates for A grade competitions at the European Commission: the Dutch ad hoc group on recruitment, The Hague 1981, unpublished, p.7.

(18) European Parliament, Document 135/77, op.cit., pp.80-8.

(19) Lawrence Scheinmann and Werner Feld, 'The EEC and National Civil Servants of Member States', International Organisation, Winter 1972, Vol.26, No.1, p.130.

(20) European Parliament, Document 135/77, op.cit., p.88.

II THE RECRUITMENT

The circumstances under which Britons were recruited to Community institutions at the enlargement of the Community in 1973 were not ideal. The importance of sending Britons of high quality to Brussels was recognised, and indeed Mr Heath was personally committed to doing so. The 'Establishment', however, within the government and outside, remained less than totally convinced of the rightness of 'going into Europe', and not wholly optimistic about Britain's future there. Politicians blew hot and cold over membership of the Community; the Labour Party was largely hostile and even Mr Heath did not have the total support of his party. In Whitehall opinions were divided and 'neutralism' towards the Community was sometimes the most positive of attitudes in some Departments. From the outset, in the general climate of uncertainty, long-term career prospects in Community institutions whose functions were anyway barely understood and whose reputations were less than dynamic were unlikely to have widespread appeal. It would have taken powerful incentives and a particularly energetic and aggressive campaign of recruitment to attract a large number of the best qualified candidates. The lack of both goes some way to explaining a disappointing outcome which contained the seeds of future difficulty. Nevertheless there were over 300 Britons of sufficiently high calibre who were willing to go to Brussels to serve in the 'A' grades of the Commission and the Council Secretariat in 1973. This chapter looks at where they were found (their previous professional backgrounds) and at some of the considerations which led them to choose to serve Europe, as well as tracing the course of the recruiting operation and reasons why it failed to attract suitable candidates in greater numbers.

The preparations

Preparations to recruit 1,000 or so Britons to the Community institutions could not begin until after Parliament's endorsement on 28 October 1971 of the decision to join the Community on the terms negotiated. Each institution was to mount its own recruiting operation, and of course retain final responsibility for appointments. The Civil Service Department (CSD) was to be responsible for liaising with their representatives and helping them find staff from inside and outside the Civil Service, with a particular emphasis on the top levels in which member governments had an acknowledged interest. The Lord Privy Seal, Lord Jellicoe, who was the Minister in day-to-day charge of the Civil Service, visited Brussels in March 1972 formally to initiate discussions on recruitment. Since the Commission was the largest employer amongst the institutions, it was the CSD's chief interlocutor, followed at some distance by the Council Secretariat. The Commission set up a unit to deal with the recruitment at enlargement within DG IX, the Personnel and Administrative Directorate-General, under the direction of a distinguished Community official, M. Daniel Strasser. The Commission's delegation in London at Kensington Palace Gardens was to have a co-ordinating role for the posts below the top levels, dispensing information, placing advertisements and sending and receiving application forms. In Whitehall a special unit in the CSD was set up under a Deputy Secretary to co-ordinate recruitment, with the Secretary to the Cabinet and the European Unit in the Cabinet Office exercising a watching brief over its activities but reluctant to be involved in staffing in detail, below the top 15 posts or so.

A joint working group of British and Community officials was also set up to work out details of selection machinery, the number and type of posts to be available, and detailed questions of conditions of service, in consultation with civil servants from the other new member states, Denmark, Ireland and, at that stage, Norway. Arrangements were set in train to increase mutual understanding, with familiarisation tours for officials on both sides of the Channel and preparations undertaken for some 100 British civil servants to spend some weeks at a time at the Commission as stagiaires.

Such mutual familiarisation was sorely needed. Responsible officials on both sides of the Channel began their task very much in the dark. In the UK there was as yet no widespread familiarity with or understanding of the workings of the Community even within the Civil Service, which, if the patterns of Community staffing established by the Six were followed, could be expected to be a major source of recruits. Those officials who knew the

26

Community best were busy with preparations for entry in the policy areas, compared to which staffing was a low-key and uncharismatic issue. The Community had been observed and reported upon, of course; seminars and lectures on its workings and its policies had been held at the Civil Service College; and a limited number of administrative trainees had already served at the UK delegation to the Community in Brussels. This was, however, different from first-hand involvement. It was acknowledged that the Commission combined French and German civil service traditions, for example, but few knew what that meant in practical terms. British officials had little idea of conditions of service or methods of appointment in an organisation run quite differently from any other international organisation; language was a problem; grading of jobs in recognisable terms was a bigger one; salaries were unknown. On the Commission side too there was little detailed familiarity amongst responsible officials with conditions and society in the UK, or with the British Civil Service. There were a few British officials already working in Community institutions but they were not appointed to run or even to advise on the recruitment, apart from those in the Commission delegation in London. In short, at the beginning there was a veritable wall of ignorance such that mistakes were difficult to avoid and perhaps inevitable. 'It was,' said one responsible official from Whitehall, 'like trying to get to the top of a mountain in a fog.'(1)

Basic misapprehensions

The CSD saw its first tasks as to try to identify vacancies to be filled, in total figures and in specific areas, to draw up suitable lists of candidates from inside and outside the Civil Service from which the Commission and other institutions could make appointments, and to establish conditions of service which provided adequate incentives to candidates of good quality. In all this it was handicapped by some basic misapprehensions arising from a lack of familiarity with the Community which threatened the success of the operation from the start.

The first concerned salaries. At a very early stage an interdepartmental working group looked at a comparison of Community salaries plus education allowances with the salaries and allowances of British diplomats and civil servants seconded to Brussels. These seemed to show that, in general, Community officials of equivalent rank would be at best no worse off, except at the top two levels where they would actually be less well remunerated. At all levels there would, it was thought, be a disincentive in that Community allowances for children's education would not cover the cost of boarding school or other fee-paying education which might be felt necessary for British children until an English language stream was developed in the Community's European School. It was agreed that great effort would be needed to remove this disincentive to attract good candidates. Considerable time and discussion at a high level was expended on this issue, with the Commission discussing the possibility of double education allowances at all grades, and a 15 per cent tax-free extra allowance for British A1 and A2 posts; but this would have entailed getting the Council of Ministers to change Community allowances, an unlikely eventuality. The British Government, incredible as it seems now, considered ways and means of introducing a possible 'hardship' allowance for top British Community officials.

It seems that the structure of Community emoluments had simply been misunderstood. Comparative remuneration is anyway a difficult area, fraught with misunderstandings, with direct national equivalents hard to calculate accurately. Suffice it to say that the high basic salary, taxed generously compared to the UK, and complemented by very adequate tax-free child allowances, an education allowance, a head of household allowance, expatriation allowances with a 'national weighting' element, brought total net income levels in the Community institutions in 1981 to something just under double those for equivalent grades in Whitehall, for example. They surprised and delighted most Britons when they actually got to Brussels and found that Commission officials were very far from being the 'chaps grateful for the odd bottle of duty-free whisky' which was one image reportedly circulating at the time of recruitment. It was a cause for great regret that the word got round in Whitehall and elsewhere that the money was not good, on top of other perceived disadvantages. Had the true scale of remuneration been realised and published, there might well have been greater interest in going to Brussels among those best qualified for jobs there.

Another basic difficulty, which primarily affected candidates from the Civil Service, was over the grading of jobs at the administrative level in the Commission. From the beginning these were inadequately assessed, reflecting perhaps Whitehall's less than enthusiastic view of the Commission and a broader and more persistent misunderstanding of the role and workings of the Commission. The CSD embarked on its recruiting operation rating an A1 as an Under-Secretary, A2 as an Assistant Secretary, A3 as a Principal and A4-7 as Principal to Higher Executive Officer. This was, as it was eventually realised, a grave under-estimation of the

28

tasks and responsibilities of most Commission officials. The difficulty probably arose from the Commission practice of having titles and grades dependent on structure rather than assessment of responsibility. Thus an A1 might be a Director-General of a front-line directorate such as Agriculture or External Affairs, with responsibilities quite as great as those of a Permanent Secretary in Whitehall, or of a small service directorate with much less pressure or scope. Titles covered a wide range of responsibility at each level and the difficulty was in assessing broad averages. It would have been better to have matched the Civil Service grade to each job, but in the circumstances of the recruitment this was not practical. As it was, Commission grades tended to be judged by standards which were often inappropriate, since they ignored the added dimension of the multinational and multilingual aspects of the Commission, where force of personality can be as important as intellectual processes, and where quite junior officials can have the responsibility of representing the Commission before the member states in formal gatherings. The extent of the difficulty about the equivalencies dawned gradually, but the damage was done. The recruitment campaign got off on the wrong foot, especially within the Civil Service, and had people aiming at the wrong targets. As a result some of the early candidates were not of sufficient experience, seniority or merit for some of the posts for which they aimed.

'Catch 22'

A third flaw in the recruiting campaign originated in Brussels where it had been decided that enlargement would not essentially change the shape of the Commission. Staff regulations were suspended for a limited period to allow the recruitment of new member state nationals at all grades and levels. At the lower levels 1,008 new posts were authorised for the new member states, but at the administrative level there was to be no big expansion and room for the new recruits was mainly to be made through a golden handshake or voluntary retirement, which eventually vacated 247 posts. The trouble was that the actual jobs vacated were not known, and could not be known, until the Commission's weeding operation had been completed, the British Commissioners appointed and their portfolios decided, and the British areas of preference and priority negotiated for and decided. The lack of central direction and detailed forward planning was perhaps an inescapable result of the nature of the Commission and its workings, but the haphazard way many posts were vacated and redistributed at the last moment militated against the success of the recruiting operation from the first.

Not knowing exactly which jobs would be available made recruiting difficult, particularly where technical expertise, which the Commission required, was an essential qualification. It was difficult to interest top quality experts, and have them processed by a selection board and standing by as candidates for jobs which remained hypothetical until the last moment. It required candidates to have particularly strong motives for going to Europe, which the climate of the times did not encourage. At the same time, if a well qualified high-powered UK candidate was standing by for a particular post, then ipso facto there was a good argument for the UK filling that post, so the considerations became circular. This 'catch 22' situation underlay, and one might almost say undermined, the recruiting operation from start to finish. In the end, at the last minute when jobs were identified it sometimes became a question of getting not the right expert for the job, but (and chiefly at the lower levels) simply the right kind of person of the right nationality into the job. This in the end suited neither the best interests of the Commission nor of the UK, resulting as it did in cases of dissatisfied fonctionnaires stuffed into unsuitable jobs. The Commission changed their procedure for Greek enlargement in 1981 as a result of their experience with the first enlargement, making sure that each Directorate-General had defined clearly every post to be filled and advertised specifically for it. This was easier to do, of course, with the smaller numbers involved.

The method
From the first the CSD concentrated on the administrative appointments to the virtual exclusion of the B, C, and D grades, except that notices of vacancies there were included in internal Civil Service circulars about posts for British staff in Community institutions. Within the A grades the aim at the A1-2 levels, which were the CSD's primary focus, was to compile short lists of suitable candidates from inside and outside the Civil Service, on the basis of nominations and informal interview boards. The British Commissioners would then select some 20-25 candidates for the top jobs using the lists, and submit them to the Commissioner or Director-General responsible for the various posts who would make the formal appointment.

At the A3 level, however, the Commission played a part in the selection procedure at an early stage. The CSD could not exclude candidates, but its recommendations were to carry weight. A top Commission official accompanied by a CSD expert was to interview candidates from a list which had undergone preliminary sifting by the CSD. The list was to be composed of non-civil servants and civil servants, both those nominated by their departments and those volunteering in internal trawls. In the event, however, many candidates who had applied direct to the Commission were interviewed without any preliminary vetting so that the CSD's filtering role here was limited. In fact, after some two months of interviewing, the Commission representative was whisked away to a cabinet job in January 1973, and some candidates were left to pursue their own candidatures direct with the Commission and British cabinet members, sometimes successfully. The appointments at this level were theoretically to be handled by the new British Commissioners, but in practice it was their cabinets who forwarded names on the basis of graded reports of the interviews to the Directors-General who made the formal appointments. Some 200 candidates, selected from lists of about 1,000, were interviewed and 47 A3s were appointed out of an estimated 50 vacancies.

Below the A3 level, the Commission ran its own selection procedures and CSD participation was limited to advice and help with finding British representatives to assist selection boards. At A4-5, respondents to advertisements and Civil Service candidates, who had to apply direct to the Commission at Kensington Palace Gardens, were not vetted or processed in any way by the CSD, unless they had been rejected by the A3 boards and advised to aim a little lower. The basic qualifications, as for all the A grades, were a degree or 'equivalent professional experience' and knowledge of one other Community language, plus a period of relevant experience which at this grade was 7 years. Candidates appeared before a board of Community officials who often, but not always, seemed to show greatest interest in a candidate's ability to understand if not to speak a second language, and tended to ask questions testing knowledge and skill in the manner of an oral examination rather than attitudes and aptitudes, in an interview which some called friendly and others perfunctory. At this level then, there was no CSD guidance on consistency of quality. Interviews with Directors-General who were to make the appointments became a basic selection procedure and at this level there was often no technical personnel expertise employed. There was thus inherent in the selection procedures a potential for uneven quality in this cadre, which also happened to be one where technical expertise was at a premium and the disadvantages of the non-specificity of jobs available fell heavily. The CSD knew little of progress at this level, only that some 2,000 application forms were sent out and that in the end there was a considerable shortfall in numbers appointed.

The CSD was extremely discouraging about the possibility of finding a sufficient number of good candidates at the A6-7 level. It felt this was an area already creamed off by the Civil Service administrative grade examinations and that a target of 70 or so appointments was ambitious. As well as a degree, candidates were expected to have one year's relevant experience. Formal written examinations were to be held, followed by an interview in a Community language other than English, run entirely by the Commission on the pattern of their normal recruitment exams at this level. A total of 658 candidates took general papers, language papers, and one of a choice of special subjects, such as law, economics, social affairs, and agriculture. The examinations were held in the Alexandra Palace in conditions of some discomfort and disorganisation, but together with the interviews produced a more than satisfactory result, with 114 successful candidates of whom 48 got more than 70 per cent, with the top two candidates being women.

Civil servants' reservations
Within the Civil Service jobs in Community institutions at any level had no widespread appeal, and it soon became apparent that, for this reason alone, there was no question of the British contingent in Brussels consisting of 75 per cent civil servants, as had been supposed by the CSD in the first weeks of their operation. There was a natural constituency in those who were supporters of the Community ideal and who now had the opportunity to work for it in person in Brussels, and in those who had personal motives for wanting to change their circumstances. Otherwise, by the nature of the profession, unless they were in the Foreign and Commonwealth Office, most civil servants, and certainly the older ones, were likely to be settled and not predisposed to go abroad. There would need to be pressing reasons for exchanging an interesting and well-paid career in a prestigious, respected and influential profession for an uncertain future in institutions for whom not many colleagues had much respect. Though it was widely understood that Mr Heath himself had affirmed that a tour in Brussels would be a key to future advancement, there could be no formal and general guarantees of good jobs in Whitehall in several years' time, and there was therefore some reluctance to be the first to put such assurances to the test. The advantages in career terms seemed hard to envisage for a man leaving the main stream of his ministry for a 'technical operation' where the terms of service were not particularly attractive. The greatest demand for quality and numbers was at the Principal level, both for the Community and at home. A Principal within sight of promotion was likely to be

reluctant to be away from base at the crucial time and run the risk of being overlooked, while young Principals, aware of the demands in the Home Civil Service for breadth of experience, were reluctant to become highly specialised in their formative years, which a tour in Brussels would entail, and so prejudice their future career at home.

The mistakes in equivalent gradings took a particular toll of those civil servants who did aspire to jobs in Brussels despite the apparent disadvantages. Some newly promoted Assistant Secretaries aimed at A2 posts, and some young Principals under 30 at A3 posts, when the existing average age of promotion even to A4 to A5 within the Commission was 43. At the other end of the scale, rather ageing Assistant Secretaries and Under-Secretaries, who had reached their ceiling at home, aspired to A1 posts. Ambitious senior officials were likely to have what interest they evinced in going to the Commission extinguished by the low rating of the top jobs; and some suitable candidates at lower levels were certainly lost to the operation when, rejected eventually on age grounds, as they had to be, they refused to accept that the next grade down was appropriate for them, because the equivalents were never amended in general circulars.

In the face of all the negative factors it was clear that 'return ticket' arrangements were vital to reassure those still interested enough to be tempted to try a change of scene for five years or so. An assured return to the Civil Service would serve two purposes, to reassure the timid but interested, and to encourage mobility between the Commission and the Civil Service and thus spread mutual familiarity and confidence. The formal Commission position was that secondments as such were not recognised, though the French had long favoured them, as we have noted, and during the recruitment period intimated again to the British that they would like to see 20 per cent of grade 'A' posts filled openly by national civil servants on secondment. As it was, the CSD worked out with the Civil Service unions arrangements to ensure that civil servants who went to Brussels were guaranteed reinstatement after up to five years away, at the substantive grade and salary at which they had left, with pensions also protected. It was also suggested from the Cabinet Office that some accelerated promotions, to Assistant Secretary for example, should be conditional on accepting a job in Brussels. The combination of a promotion and guaranteed return at that rank was an incentive offered, however, only to a few, who were deemed particularly suitable Brussels material.

33

On the whole, the CSD proceeded in a conventional and somewhat low-key fashion to gather the names of potential Civil Service recruits. There was no question of its mounting a dynamic imaginative campaign, with Establishment Officers approaching the brightest and the best in their departments with a glowing picture of the attractions of a career in Europe, even had such a picture been credible. Departments were circulated for volunteers, and Establishment Officers were asked for nominations of suitable candidates for the top jobs. Below A3, candidates were told to apply to the Commission direct. Busy Establishment Officers were thus asked to supply good candidates for what was often perceived as the remote and difficult area of Europe, not always recognised as useful to the home department, while at the same time Under-Secretaries in their own departments were pressing them for good candidates for urgent jobs. Apathy and resistance was a not uncommon reaction to the European option in the departments; they did not want to see their best young people go to Brussels and had difficulty in visualising how they could be fitted in if they returned. Some rare Establishment Officers did recognise that it was in the department's long-term best interests to nominate good people, but in general, as is so often the case, the urgent took precedence over the important and it was the demands of importunate Under-Secretaries which took precedence. At the same time, the first Civil Service lists were undeniably used by some Establishment Officers as a convenient resting place for their awkward squad, a collecting place for dead wood, though the CSD weeding of the lists later in the year went some way to correct this.

The private sector
The Civil Service was only one source of potential recruits, however. It was rapidly borne in upon ministers that other organisations with an interest in Europe wanted to see some of their people recruited, to be sure they had contact points in their areas of interest and a chance to learn how the system worked. In the face of increasing pressures from the Trades Union Congress, the Confederation of British Industry, big companies like the oil giants and banking and insurance, and from ministers and the press, the idea of an overwhelming complement of civil servants fell by the wayside. The Commission also made it clear that they needed the expertise and first-hand experience which private sector candidates could bring. The Lord Privy Seal himself was keen to 'strike a balance' between numbers of civil servants and outsiders. He was active in trying to enlist good recruits, tapping an informal consultative network through regular working lunches with

34

influential leading personalities from the City, the universities, the nationalised industries and private industry.   The CBI and TUC were asked to submit lists of potential candidates for the A1-3 level, and the CBI circulated some 60 large firms with international interests asking them for nominations.   The CSD asked government departments to explore their contacts in the industries with which they dealt for suitable nominations, and itself dredged the fabled file of the 'great and good' for likely material, though to little effect.   There were also the pro-Community academic community and the 'European lobby' to be trawled for candidates. Meanwhile the CSD also maintained a register of unsolicited applications, of which as early as December 1971 there were already 69 ranging from retired generals to academics and likely figures from the City.   By December 1972 this list had grown to about 1,000, but it was thought that only a small minority could be considered likely material.   The CSD's role was to examine all the names thrown up by these means, and with the aid of advice from people in the departments who might know the individuals concerned, measure them against internal candidates for inclusion on the A1-3 lists to be submitted to the Commission.

At first the response was disappointing.   The private sector no less than the public viewed the Community with suspicion and through the lens of ignorance.   Though there was a reservoir of pro-Europe enthusiasts, and some big firms like Shell and the other oil companies encouraged extremely good candidates to come forward, many of the same restraints which inhibited good civil service candidates from applying operated with perhaps greater force in the private sector.   Why should a successful businessman throw up a good career to take a chance in a multinational bureaucracy, if he was not a Europhile or had no personal motives for going abroad?   Moreover, there was not often a return ticket to tempt the timid.   Good potential candidates, once identified, were certainly deterred by the 'catch 22' element of the whole affair. Not untypical was the case of the man, invited three times to apply at the A3 level for a 'possible vacancy', who refused each time, but was eventually prevailed upon to accept an outright offer of the specific post for which he was eminently suited: he did so, out of a sense of public duty and conscious of taking a risk, unaware even of the eventual financial advantages.   His proved a most successful and happy appointment.

Common difficulties
The hurdles outlined by the Commissioner responsible for Personnel in the debate in the European Parliament quoted in Chapter I (p.23)

were common to candidates from the public and private sectors alike. Chief amongst them was the necessity for a 'satisfactory knowledge' of at least one of the Community languages in addition to English. Mr Heath had promised President Pompidou at the Summit of May 1971 that the British contingent would be competent in French, but despite the promise of language training for candidates, and the effects within the Civil Service of the recently instituted exchange programme with the Ecole Nationale d'Administration, the language problem loomed large for many aware of the deficiencies of their schoolboy French. It loomed large, on the other hand, for recruiters too, aware of the possibility that this extra dimension could get out of proportion. In the opinion of one recruiter, 'It was like checking to see if a man had a bicycle with which to get to work - the tendency became to give him a job if he had one, forgetting to check whether he was actually the best man for the job.'

The domestic aspects of a move abroad also presented difficulties. Wives' careers and life styles were not necessarily transferable. The education of children presented potential problems when the European School had not yet started its English stream, the British School of Brussels was a virtually unknown new enterprise and British boarding schools were not known to be affordable. There was a need for basic information about life in Belgium for people considering a move; information about such details as tax, moving costs, housing, insurance and simply 'what life was like'. There was then, of course, no pool of experience on which those contemplating an application could draw, or easily reached contacts such as were available to those who applied in later years. The CSD eventually produced a booklet Brussels Briefing on these sorts of subjects for the first pioneers, and the Commission also prepared material on officials' rights and obligations and on conditions of life in Brussels; but some of this kind of information could usefully and fairly easily have been made available to potential candidates at an earlier stage.

Underlying much of the reluctance to apply, however, was the uncertainty over Britain's commitment to the Community in the circumstances of the Labour Party's decision to boycott the institutions and left-wing opposition to the Community itself. At one point the lack of suitable candidates seemed so severe that a CSD recruiter was quoted as joking despairingly that the main requirements for prospective British Eurocrats were an ability to speak French and a willingness to go to Brussels.

36

There can be little doubt that the recruiting net, especially outside the Civil Service, was not cast as widely as it might have been, giving the impression that the recruiting was something of a closed shop operation. There were articles in newspapers from time to time about the opportunities for employment in Community institutions,(2) as well as the advertisements of the vacancies themselves, placed in a range of newspapers from October 1972.(3) Undoubtedly many likely areas were left untapped, however, and even some of the most obvious ones slipped at first between the two stools of the CBI and the CSD lists. The list-making procedure itself was not necessarily the most appropriate way of approaching nominations at the top levels, a personal approach at board level being perhaps more likely to yield candidates of appropriate stature from the private sector. Commission observers remarked that though they found the CSD open-minded and full of goodwill, they did feel that it tended to dramatise and over-complicate the problems of recruitment, and that by comparison with the French it tended to be rather passive in its recruitment methods. It is hard not to disagree. Certainly some six months after the start of operations the CSD Minister was worrying about the leisurely pace at which affairs were proceeding, and the operation was punctuated by hortatory memoranda from the Cabinet Office. CSD officials themselves in retrospect regretted the lack of resources and time to encourage individuals of the right calibre. On the other hand, the Civil Service Commission complained about the unco-ordinated and wasteful nature of Community recruitment methods. The depths of the unfamiliarity among officials in Brussels with appropriate means of reaching the A4-7 recruits for whom they were solely responsible was demonstrated by the first drafts of their recruitment advertisements, which appalled the CSD officials who had the task of tactfully amending them.

The Council Secretariat
A prime example of the lack of co-ordination remarked by the CSD was the way in which the smaller Community institutions recruited separately from each other. The Council Secretariat, for example, ran an entirely separate recruitment operation from the Commission, though it was looking for personnel with only slightly differing skills and was likely to find them from the same sources, and especially at the top three levels from the Civil Service lists. It was not uncommon to find candidates applying for both institutions. The Council's needs were more modest than the Commission's, with some 30 staff at the A grades to be found from the UK. The upheaval involved in making posts available for the

37

new member states was magnified by the close-knit nature of the organisation resulting from its comparatively small size. Perhaps because of this the Council was slow to get its recruiting programme under way. Its methods paralleled those of the Commission, but its task was more difficult; if the Commission and its activities were not widely known or understood, the Council was even less so. Moreover, by oversight or mismanagement advertisements for A grade vacancies appeared in UK newspapers at scarcely the best time - on Christmas Eve. Mr Kenneth Christofas was appointed in January 1973, as the most senior Briton, to be one of the six Directors-General. It was a particularly suitable appointment as he had most recently been Deputy Secretary in charge of the European Co-ordination Department in the Cabinet Office, and had been Deputy Head of the British Delegation to the EEC between 1969 and 1972. Other vacancies in the top ranks remained unfilled, however, and with few suitable candidates, until a senior official in the UK Representation to the Community took the initiative in drawing the vacancies to the attention of some well qualified colleagues he knew to be interested in Community service.

The Commissioners appointed

The Commissioners were appointed in October 1972, Sir Christopher Soames from the Conservative Party and George Thomson from the Labour Party. They first selected their personal staff or cabinets. Sir Christopher Soames, fresh from his experience as Ambassador in Paris, leaned towards FCO personnel and in selecting David Hannay as his Chef de Cabinet chose one of those with the greatest experience of the Community, well placed to identify posts of potential influence there, and described by The Economist as 'a vigorous operator ... skilled in the workings of the Brussels machine'(4). George Thomson leavened his FCO intake with his Chef de Cabinet, Gwyn Morgan, who had been Assistant General Secretary of the Labour Party and 'a master of brokering Labour Party power'(5). The influence of the cabinets on the selection of the A3 and even the A2 posts was to be considerable, and the contrast in styles and political allegiance between the two Commissioners and their Cabinets was reflected in the sometimes differing kinds of person they succeeded in appointing. It was held that the Soames cabinet tended to think first of recruits from Whitehall, while George Thomson through Gwyn Morgan looked to people in Labour politics and industry, and is credited with mining the seam of Welsh talent, the 'Tafia', which has made its mark within the Commission. Through their Minister the CSD was put in touch with the Commissioners and briefed them on progress so far.

There was now a working assumption that the UK would field 18.7 per cent of Commission staff, of which 297 would be A grade, 5 A1, 19 A2, 51 A3, 152 A4-5 and 70 A6-7. Coincidentally there was a change of the Deputy Secretary in charge of the operation in London.

Meanwhile, as the CSD had been compiling its lists, Ministers had been identifying key areas of interest in the Commission. They decided that first in order of importance were economic and monetary policy, industrial policy, external trade relations, regional policy and agriculture. Ranked second priority were transport (later upgraded), science and technology, and aid to developing countries. Depending on the portfolios of her Commissioners, Britain was to aim to contribute a Director-General or at least a Deputy Director-General in each of the five key areas. An interdepartmental working party had gone further, circulating departments to identify the chief areas of interest to them and the jobs which Britons could most usefully fill in Brussels, in order to establish a draft order of priorities.

The CSD had hoped to be able to put before the Commissioners two or three names for each of the six DG posts and for each of the Director posts in the priority areas, and the same for the second order posts, with a total of some 75 candidates to fill some 24 jobs. The Commissioners were to interview jointly all candidates at the A1 level and all candidates at the A2 level between them, preferably in the first week in December. The first Director-General appointments were due to be made on 10 January. Though the Civil Service candidates at this level for the top priority posts had been shortlisted by six weeks before this date (and few outside candidates considered suitable had appeared by this stage) the CSD was admitting with concern that it was some way from being able to finalise its lists. The names for second order posts at this level had not been processed and replies from a third and wider interdepartmental trawl for the non-priority areas were still awaited. Unease mounted with the Commissioners' reaction to the lists they did receive. Their expectations may well have been unrealistically high, given the unfavourable climate of the time, but they were unhappy with the quality of the candidates on the first A1 and A2 lists and were concerned to see the lists for A3 and to have some idea of the quality of the field for A4-5 and A6-7. Considerable disappointment was expressed to the Lord Privy Seal at the lack of progress in identifying suitable people for high level appointments, and doubts were voiced as to whether preliminary sifting of candidates had been adequate or whether the net had been cast wide enough. It was considered odd, to say the least, that, for example, the only candidate for one important A2 post was someone near retirement age who had had only a day or two's warning that he was under consideration for Brussels.

The CSD was now down to offering one name per expected post, i.e. 24 names, but still hoped to produce two in the case of A1 posts for priority DGs. The rejection of a number of candidates by the Commissioners holding their interviews in Old Admiralty Buildings left holes which had to be plugged very rapidly, and each day counted. The new Deputy Secretary worked very hard indeed, telephoning people to persuade them to apply, getting Permanent Secretaries to put up strong candidates and rousing Establishment Officers to renewed vigour with pressure from the Cabinet Office. Better lists were put together, improved in quality and quantity. The Commissioners urgently tapped their contacts, the Lord Privy Seal his, and influential figures in industry, commerce and the City were rallied, at this late stage, into actively and urgently producing ideas and suggestions. A certain discreet pressure was applied to reluctant but otherwise suitable candidates, with persuasive phone calls from the Cabinet Office or a Permanent Secretary, invitations to the House of Lords for a drink and a chat, and suggestions that the Governor of the Bank of England might be 'disappointed' if City figures declined to be available. The result of this last-minute reaching out for candidates was that at the end of January when the smoke cleared after the negotiation of Commission portfolios and the haggling over the A1-A2 posts began, there were Britons on the list described as 'of appropriate standing' to fill those jobs, from an appropriate range of backgrounds, and not disproportionately from the Civil Service.

Top posts and appointments
Once the Commissioners had secured their portfolios of External Affairs and Regional Policy, which the UK Government and the respective Commissioners welcomed, negotiations began in Brussels for the Director-General and Deputy Director-General posts. The Director-General posts to be filled by Britons were in the Industry and Transport Directorates-General, which had been top priority targets, Social Affairs (an unexpected but welcome vacancy for which no candidate was standing by), and Dissemination of Information (which had been low on the list of priorities but was not unwelcome). Deputy Director-General posts were in Agriculture and Development Aid, with a Deputy Secretary-General post which had been second order priority but which was recognised as important. This was considered a fair spread of posts

and those concerned were reasonably content. The chief regret was that it had not been possible to get a senior post in Economic and Financial Affairs. Industry turned out to be something of a disappointment, in the absence of a Community industry policy. Within four years however, it had been exchanged for a Director-General post in Energy, and Social Affairs was later also exchanged for External Relations when the latter was no longer in a British Commissioner's portfolio; thus what the negotiators had regarded as an unexciting but satisfactory range of jobs at top levels filled by UK nationals was converted before too long to a thoroughly satisfactory one.

The first appointments to these jobs proved to be of mixed success. A leading industrialist, Ronnie Grierson, aged 51, was put in charge of Industry, persuaded, it was said, to go to Brussels by Mr Heath himself. He reputedly found the Commission totally unsuited to his dynamic style, and left in early 1974. After an interval of many months, he was replaced, in the post of Director General of Energy, by Leonard Williams, a former Deputy Secretary for EEC and International Affairs in the Department of Energy. Michael Shanks, aged 45, a journalist, economist and industrialist, was plucked from his new job as a director of British Oxygen, apparently at George Thomson's suggestion, to be Director General of Social Affairs in DG V. He too found the bureaucratic process tortuous, experiencing difficulty with his Irish Commissioner and cabinet. Conscious that his former job could not remain open for his return for ever, he left at the end of 1975, bequeathing his job to a waiting Belgian. Raymond Le Goy, aged 53, a former Under Secretary in Civil Aviation at the Department of Trade and Industry, was appointed to head DG VII, Transport, and the slate was completed with the appointment to DG XIII of Raymond Appleyard, aged 51, a former senior official already at the Commission, whose appointment was also an opportunity for the British Government to show that those serving in the Commission before enlargement were not now to be forgotten. The Deputy Secretary-General job went to a highly regarded ex-diplomat and Europhile of long standing, Christopher Audland, aged 46, who later went on to follow Leonard Williams as Director-General of Energy in 1981. The important Agriculture job went to an exceptionally well qualified and able Ministry of Agriculture official, who had been in charge of entry negotiations on agriculture, Michael Franklin, who at 45 had already been an Under-Secretary for some four years and achieved promotion to Deputy Secretary on his return to Whitehall. The post of Deputy Director-General in DG VIII went to Maurice Foley, an ex-Labour MP and

41

former Foreign Office Minister with considerable experience of African Affairs.

The negotiations for the Director jobs at A2 and the A3 posts involved long and detailed discussions conducted chiefly at chef de cabinet level. The chefs, with CSD lists in hand, tried to match influential jobs, well distributed within the Commission, with the best candidates. The negotiations were tough, requiring a keen sense of which were the posts of greatest interest, and stamina to continue the hard bargaining late into the night. As one newspaper headline put it succinctly, if over dramatically, 'Britain's market fixers spill blood'(6). The A2 jobs were distributed and filled by the end of January. Some 20 posts were filled by Britons, in the Legal Service, the Statistical Office and the Customs Union, and in the Directorates-General dealing with External Trade, Industry, Economic and Financial Affairs, Competition, Agriculture, Development, Social Affairs, Personnel, Press and Information, Training and Education, Energy, Credit and Investment, Banking and Insurance, and the Budget. The spread of jobs was considered reasonably satisfactory, and the people to fill them came from backgrounds sufficiently varied to satisfy the requirements of the Commissioners and the preference of the British authorities.

The A3 appointments

The A3 operation was mostly completed by the end of March, with the cabinets still continuing to conduct negotiations for desirable posts and making appointments, lists in hand, as new names came in and new jobs became vacant with former officials retiring and lists of preferences for A3 jobs still appearing from Whitehall. Some confusion and uncertainty was perhaps inevitable as people retired from the Commission and new people arrived. Perhaps the most extreme example is one candidate's story of how, nominated and cleared for an A3 appointment after a CSD trawl of the Quangos, he had forwarded his papers for confirmation to Brussels in June and was told not to go on holiday in August because he might be needed then. In October he heard that his papers had been locked away in a desk by an official taking voluntary retirement, and had not been discovered until his replacement arrived. By this time someone else had been appointed to 'his' job. He eventually took an A4 post to be promoted to A3 some five years later.

As the urgency and interest of policy matters pressed in increasingly, the personnel placement side grew progressively more burdensome. Individuals were also now allowed to pursue their own candidatures direct. It had been a somewhat incongruous and divisive, if necessary and inevitable, start to full European partnership to be haggling in a nationalist corner for British interests, and some of those most directly involved felt this keenly. There was no doubt that it was a relief to those concerned to be able to draw a line beneath the operation, with 47 posts obtained. If there were regrets at what was achieved at this level, they centred not so much on the number as on the quality of some of the jobs obtained. It was counted as a success to have filled as many as six A3 posts in DG VI, Agriculture, but of the six only one could really be described as a 'frontline' or functional post, that of supervising fruit and vegetables and processed products, the others being in areas such as research and forestry, and of less direct interest. There were regrets later too, that the principle had been accepted that in DG VIII, the Development Directorate, since the British had joined the Community too late to be a party to the Yaounde Agreement, it would be improper to have Britons in posts dealing with it. The argument seemed specious in retrospect and its acceptance left a legacy of British under-representation in an important area which was hard to dissipate. It was at this, the A3, level also where the mistake over equivalent grades in the Civil Service had an influence in getting men much younger than their peers from the Six positioned over experienced and able men some ten or fifteen years their senior, with consequent management problems for some of the new arrivals of such intensity that they were felt to militate against some successful long-term careers in the Commission. This was the highest level at which a British woman was appointed, Liliana Archibald, who went to DG I to be in charge of export credits.

Grades A4-A7
Below the A3 level candidates were on their own, and here the idiosyncratic Commission method of recruiting, the full implications of which were generally unknown in the UK, and unexplained to candidates, took its toll. Those who had passed the concours, whether A4-5 or A6-7 (and some passed both and were offered jobs at both levels), were placed on lists of those 'deemed suitable for employment'. There was no central direction or internal liaison over these lists. Directors perused them and called for interview those candidates who seemed most suitable for the vacancies they had to fill, and they tended to do this at short notice but over an extended period. Thus, often after bewildering weeks or months of silence candidates might get summoned to Brussels the next day. Of course many could not go, and some found themselves summoned more than once by different Directorates-General

within the space of weeks. Since there was a particularly lengthy procedure for allowing expenses, some were inconvenienced and actually inhibited by the cost.(7) Moreover, some arrived in Brussels to find no interview board convened or that they had been given the wrong date. The most notorious case was that of a candidate working in Fiji who replied to an urgent summons for interview to find not only that the board had met the day before the date he had been given, but also that his travel expenses were only likely to be paid from the nearest Community country to his port of embarkation, that is from Italy. (Another candidate from Mauritius was more astute or better informed, and had his expenses paid from a nearby French Overseas Department. He went on to have one of the most distinguished and interesting careers of all the Britons in the junior A grades, with an almost unheard-of two promotions in seven years.)

Long weeks of silence could elapse after the interviews too, so that candidates with families and commitments had sometimes started new jobs before a telegram arrived offering them a job, or even two telegrams with two jobs. In fact the most effective way of securing a suitable and desirable job (now as then) was to go to Brussels and lobby for oneself, knocking on doors and presenting oneself and one's credentials as persuasively as possible and talking to people to find out where possible vacancies might be. This was not easy for the average Briton to do (and was certainly alien to Civil Service candidates), and very few people knew enough about the Commission and how it worked to have any idea of doing it. A few who had worked in Brussels, or had connections in the Commission, did know the secret, but this was simply a matter of chance. The CSD apparently had not realised the implications of this aspect of the recruitment process and could not alert candidates to it anyway, but it did notice with concern that people were withdrawing their candidatures at the last minute and finding themselves considered for jobs in unexpected areas. There can be little doubt that a proportion of candidates fell by the wayside at this stage, and that the subsequent shortfall in A4-5 numbers owed something to these vagaries of the selection method.

It was at the A4-5 level too where the confusion over vacancies provided by the voluntary retirement scheme was greatest, and as the number of remaining candidates declined, so too did jobs. They had after all been created in a confusing way resulting from retirements, sideways moves, reorganisations and promotions, so that it was difficult as the year went on to keep track of them. It was an added complication that the voluntary retirement scheme

44

was open until 1 July, so that posts available could not be finalised until after that. There was a suspicion too that some Directors-General quietly hoarded job slots against 'contingencies' and did not try to fill them. By November, when it seemed that some 45-50 jobs at this level might be unfilled, the cabinet member with a watching brief tried to get the special recruiting period extended, and solutions were discussed, such as the appointment of numbers of agents temporaires, who had not undergone the formal selection process. When, on closer examination, there seemed to be not more than 25 and not less than ten vacancies likely, it did not seem worth going for derogation in the face of the opposition of the Secretary-General, and the idea was dropped. However in January 1974, the shortfall turned out to be 43, or about a third.

Even at the A6-7 level, where new posts were created and where there had been a surplus of 44 candidates on the 'deemed suitable for employment' lists, there turned out to be a small shortfall by the end of the year. This was not regarded as serious, however, because further concours were expected under normal conditions, in 1974. In the event, however, the political developments of 1974/5, when the referendum cast an immediate shadow of doubt over continued UK membership of the Community, led to a near total absence of recruitment of Britons and the shortfall, like that at the A4-5 levels, was not in fact made up. Indeed, both shortfalls worsened in the next two years of referendum and renegotiations as the faint hearts or failures at the Commission went home and were not necessarily replaced by other Britons. The implications of the deficiencies in numbers, and a certain unevenness in quality too, were appreciated at the time in the Cabinet Office in Whitehall and in the cabinets of the British Commissioners in Brussels, but it was simply not appropriate or possible in the next two years, with the threat of withdrawal pending, to argue credibly for special measures to make them good.

The recruitment had been bedevilled by misunderstanding and misinformation, hampered by Community methods which were not appropriate to this scale of exercise, and always in the shadow of a commitment to Community membership which seemed uncertain and was reflected in a reluctance among many potential recruits from Whitehall and outside to beat a path to Brussels and Community institutions there. Who then were the brave souls or bold spirits who were willing to take the risk or seize the opportunity, depending on the point of view, of employment in the Community, and how did they compare with colleagues already established there?

45

Sources of recruits

Neither the Community institutions nor, except at the top two levels, the CSD, analysed at the time the professional backgrounds of the recruits from the new member states. The CSD did not, for some years, even keep a central record of which civil servants from which departments had gone to Community institutions, even though they had return tickets. It is possible, however, to make some reasonable generalisations about the proportions of British recruits to the Commission coming from different kinds of backgrounds, using unofficial assessments made in 1974 by an official in the Personnel Directorate General, DG IX, making contingency plans in case of a British withdrawal after the referendum, and records kept by officials in the private offices of the British Commissioners keeping an eye on developing patterns at the time of recruitment.

The public sector

In both the Commission and the Council the majority of the British fonctionnaires came from the wider public sector as a whole. The largest single source of recruitment was the Civil Service, as had been expected, though the popular impression that ex-civil servants were to be in an overwhelming majority seems to have been far from the truth. In 1973 half the British officials in the top two grades of the Commission came from the Civil Service. This proportion has increased as top-level appointees from outside the Civil Service have dropped out to be replaced by those from inside, so that by 1980 only 2 out of 7 British A1s did not come from Whitehall. In 1973 at A2 about half, and at A3 just under half, came from the Civil Service; at A4-5 it was about a third, with considerably fewer at A6-7. Altogether civil servants seem to have constituted about a third of the British contingent.

Civil servants went to Community institutions from the whole range of departments, from HMSO and the Treasury to the Property Services Agency and the Cabinet Office. The highest proportion went predictably from departments where the experience and technical expertise was most relevant to the needs of the Community institution involved. Thus, the Ministry of Agriculture, Fisheries and Food features as the largest recruiting ground for the Commission among Whitehall departments, followed by Customs and Excise, Inland Revenue, and the Department of Trade and Industry. Even excluding the cabinets where there has usually been a strong FCO presence, the FCO was well represented among recruits, especially in the higher ranks of the Council Secretariat where perhaps the traditional diplomatic skills had a particular relevance. The Ministry of Overseas Development featured too, though to a lesser extent, with personnel going at A3 to the Council and to the Commission's Development Directorate-General, DG VIII. Perhaps for rather special reasons, influenced by the civil disorders, there was quite a sizeable recruitment from the Northern Ireland Office, of at least a dozen, who filled posts at all the grades from A2 down. Senior British lawyers in the Commission's Legal Services came from government, from the Departments of the Environment and of Health and Social Security, and in the Council Secretariat from the FCO. Indeed, there was a significant recruitment from the specialist classes within the Civil Service, reflecting the Commission's particular need for specialists rather than generalists. In A4-5 alone, almost half the 33 ex-home civil servants in the Commission were specialists - accountants, statisticians, veterinary officers and doctors.

International or overseas civil servants formed a sizeable proportion, some 10 per cent. Two heads of division came to Brussels from OECD in Paris, one to go to the Council Secretariat and the other to DG II in the Commission, while a recruit from EFTA took the highest post given to a Briton in the Competition Directorate-General. Some half dozen Britons followed the example set by the French Secretary-General of the Commission, Emile Noel, in 1958 (9) and left the Council of Europe for the Community institutions, to jobs at A3 and below. An A2 came to the Development DG from the Commonwealth Secretariat. Two recruits from the World Bank headed divisions in the Environmental and Consumer Protection Service and the Regional Policy Directorate-General, at the young age of 32 when the average A3 age in the Commission of the Six had been 48. Another came to the Commission's Legal Service from the Legal Department of the UN Secretariat. Community institutions provided a welcome opportunity to continue in public service for a number of former overseas civil servants and ex-colonial officials fairly recently retired from the newly independent Commonwealth states. Having held sometimes very senior posts there, they were able to bring their expertise to bear, chiefly at A4 level and below, and often in DG VIII where experience of the Anglophone Third World countries was notably lacking.

The reorganisation of local government was one factor which led some local government officers to consider a radical change of career, and their technical expertise and experience often in the personnel or financial field made them strong candidates. Over half a dozen went chiefly to the middle grades to A4 and A5. The

47

nationalised industries and organisations such as the Milk
Marketing Board with close contacts with government departments
were a natural fishing ground of relevant expertise easily trawled
by the CSD, through the industries' contacts with relevant
ministries. Recruits from the Central Electricity Generating
Board and the National Coal Board found niches at A3 and below in
the Energy Directorate-General, joining an A2 from the Atomic
Energy Authority. The British Steel Corporation sent former
executives to the Commission and to the Council at the A3 level,
and an ex-Assistant Secretary personnel director at the Post Office
went to the A2 post in the Commission's Personnel Directorate-
General.

A comparatively large contingent came from the academic world
or from semi-academic bodies such as the Federal Trust for
Education and Research. Accession gave some longtime supporters
of Europeanism a chance to further their cause even more directly
and in senior positions within the Commission. Some sources of
recruitment in this area were again predictable. Sussex University,
with its centre for Contemporary European Studies, fielded an A2
(formerly the Director of the Centre) and an A3 as well as more
junior recruits; Manchester sent two academics from its Extra-
Mural Department alone, including a professor to an A3 post. The
Centre for European Industrial Studies at Bath had already seen the
departure of Christopher Layton to the Commission before
accession and now lost another director to the Statistical Office.
A Briton working for the ILO in Turin took up an A4 post and other
university teachers came from a wide variety of universities, from
Coleraine (to the Council), from Queen's University, Belfast, from
Aberdeen, Exeter and London to a variety of posts and grades
between A4 and A7. The former secretary of the Committee of
Vice-Chancellors and Principals of UK Universities went as an A2
to direct education and training and cultural questions in DG XII.
A few former school teachers made up the proportion to around 10
per cent.

The private sector
The large minority, estimated to be 40 per cent, who came from
the private sector tended to be concentrated in the middle or
junior grades. The single largest contingent came from industry,
from small businesses as well as large, but most often it seems
from the big, often multinational corporations such as Sperry Rand,
Honeywell, Unilever, Metal Box, or Rothmans. The big oil
companies were a particularly fruitful recruiting ground at the
head of division level, as were the large chemical companies.

Many from industry seem to have been middle managers who came to A4-5 posts, often from firms in the UK feeling the effects of the unfavourable economic climate. The recruitment took place when the cold winds of recession were beginning to bite and prospects for many companies did not look good. The British economy was in a trough which loomed deep and large for those middle managers in industry threatened by shutdowns, takeovers, mergers and contractions, and which prompted some with experience of their effects to use their expertise in a different context. The Commission had a real need of their first-hand knowledge of industrial procedures and conditions. Enlargement was the opportunity and occasion for a transfusion and updating of practical knowledge into the middle levels of the Commission staff.

The City and the world of banking provided some distinguished recruits at the top levels, notably John Nash at A2 in DG II (Economic and Financial Affairs), and Robin Hutton and Liliana Archibald at A3 in DG XV (Financial Institutions and Taxation) and DG I (External Relations) respectively. But not many seem to have gone in at the more junior levels. A sizeable contingent came from the professions, 17 at A4-5; these were often lawyers, economists and accountants, plus some half-dozen journalists. Some came from professional or trade associations. The director of the Federation of Bakers came to an A3 post, as did a departmental secretary of the Royal Institute of Chartered Surveyors, while a former secretary of the Chartered Land Agents' Society was recruited at A4. Few trade union officials were recruited, perhaps predictably in view of the attitude of most trade unionists to the Community; Jack Peel of the National Union of Dyers, Bleachers and Textile Workers, who came in as an A2 in DG V, was the only professional trade unionist to join the Commission. Another potential recruit from the unions had eventually declined a high level appointment. For the rest, it is hard to categorise. Numbers were made up by people with a variety of backgrounds who, at A6-7 especially, tended to have had some particular, often academic or professional, contact with the Community and its institutions.

Comparisons in the Commission

The incompleteness and tentative nature of the information on the backgrounds of British recruits, as well as difficulties in comparative definitions, make any direct comparisons with the backgrounds of existing officials and any firm conclusions unreliable. However, in 1972, before the enlargement, the Commission produced an analysis of the former professional backgrounds of the A grades.(8) It showed that overall more than 50 per cent had come from the national administrations of the Six, together with 23 per cent from the private sector, 13 per cent from professional associations and trade unions, and 5 per cent, largely in the A6-7 grades, sans profession (see Table 2.1). In particular the analysis showed that 67 per cent of the top two grades came from the national administrations, 48 per cent of the A3 grade, 43 per cent of the A4-5 and 25 per cent of the A6-7. The pattern of the British ex-civil servant presence in the Commission soon after enlargement, declining with the level of grade, seems to match that established by the old Six, though the proportions are smaller. Ex-civil servants seem to have comprised about a third of Britons going to the Commission, as we have seen, joining the 50 per cent of ex-civil servants from the Six. An analysis of the percentage of A grade people in the Commission from national administrations by nationality made in 1965(9), while again not directly comparable, showed that their presence then varied from an Italian low of 52 per cent (said to reflect partly the less highly developed administration in Italy) to a West German high of 71 per cent, and an average of 66 per cent. The apparent scale of the differences between the British Civil Service presence and that of other member states, while it remains to be confirmed, is interesting. It may well reflect the undeniably less positive attitude to the Community in Whitehall in 1973, compared to that prevailing in the national administrations of the Six in the period of major recruitment, when European idealism was high and career prospects in the Commission seemed particularly attractive, as well as the deterrent effects of mistakes over comparative grading and remuneration.

The Commission's study went on to analyse the educational background of 1,000 fonctionnaires. For such information on the British intake we have to rely on the evidence produced in interviews with a 15 per cent random sample of A grade British officials.(10) The Commission's 1972 survey found that 28 per cent then had degrees in Law, 14 per cent in Economics, 10 per cent in Political Science. 30 per cent had autres diplomes universitaires (Lettres, Sciences, Agronomes, Ingenieurs etc), while 10 per cent had etudes universitaires non achevees and eight per cent no university education. Of the small British group studied, three had 'equivalent professional qualifications' rather than degrees (and of these two were senior ex-civil servants) and of the rest, Economics featured as a main topic in a third of the degrees, followed by languages (a quarter), and then Law, History, Politics and European Studies. Only two had degrees in pure or applied Sciences and at the

Table 2.1   Backgrounds of officials 'A' grades in the Commission, 1972 (%)

	National Civil Service	Private sector	Professional association or unions	Semi-public sector employees	Without employment	Public sector employees	% of total 'A' grades
A1	67	25	8				2
A2	67	12	18	3			6
A3	48	23	24	3	1.5	0.5	19
A4–5	43	24	28	1.90	2.25	0.85	50
A6–7	25	29	21.25	3	21	0.75	23

Source: Commission Paper IX A 336: 26 April 1972.

three in Agriculture. It is still the case that continental Europeans tend to do best in the Legal specialism in the A6-7 concours, while the British excel in the Economics specialism in greater numbers than candidates of other nationalities (see Appendix V). In fact, judging by the sample, the British contingent were a highly educated group. Sixty per cent of them had recorded postgraduate study (20 per cent at foreign institutes of higher education), a quarter held second degrees, 10 per cent had doctorates and 15 per cent had postgraduate professional qualifications. Almost half had their first degrees from Oxford and Cambridge, with graduates of London (most often the London School of Economics) and the Scottish universities next most numerous. Three of the survey group had achieved their degrees (and two of them had postgraduate degrees too) through adult or part-time study at technical college.

Factors influencing recruits

Whatever their professional and educational background, however, it seems that comparatively few Britons went to work in Community institutions who had not had either experience of living, working or studying abroad, or family connections with Europe or elsewhere, or previous contact with the Community. Names are a notoriously misleading guide to nationality throughout the Community, and, in the pattern of other nationalities, the list of Britons serving in the Commission contains some startlingly un-British names which suggest family origins outside the UK. Their owners not infrequently turn out to be immigrants or children of immigrants, frequently Polish or German, often Jewish refugees. Such people tend to have a familiarity with languages and an acceptance of other cultures, together sometimes with an ideal of European unity born of their families' experience, and a less insular outlook than many Britons, which make them likely to be willing and suitable recruits to the service of Europe.

Others with foreign connections less obvious than their names suggested also shared characteristics predisposing them towards service abroad. Turning again for evidence to our survey group, about a third of them had either lived abroad, usually in continental Europe, or were already spending a considerable part of their working life abroad when recruited. A quarter had spouses, and 15 per cent had parents, who did not originate in the UK, and over a third were familiar with the Community either through direct work experience or living in Brussels. Only 10 per cent had no such experience or connections before recruitment. The younger recruits in particular tended to have had direct involvement with

Community institutions. A third (4 out of 12) of the A6-7 survey group had served as <u>stagiaires</u> in the Commission, two had studied at the College of Europe at Bruges and half had degrees or a record of postgraduate study in specifically European Studies subjects.

An existing orientation towards 'abroad', and often specifically Europe, was clearly one factor encouraging many towards service in the Community institutions. A certain idealism, a desire to play a role in 'Europe stitching', was also probably present to varying degrees in the majority of recruits. Over 60 per cent of the survey group, whatever their previous experience and connections, owned to long-existing pro-European Community feelings, though only a small minority had actually belonged to pro-Community lobby groups. Over half (57 per cent) admitted that dissatisfaction with their jobs, promotion or career prospects had played a major role in their decision to make a radical change in their lives. This large proportion must reflect the effect of the contemporary economic climate in Britain on perceived career prospects, and the fact that people who are happy and successful in their careers are not likely to change unless there are powerful motives such as dedicated Europhilism and confidence in the experience enhancing career prospects in the long term, and also the existence of a safety net in the form of return tickets if the venture fails.

Scales of remuneration were an acknowledged attraction for about half of those interviewed in the survey (49 per cent), but only three (six per cent) knew exactly how much net income to expect; a third (34 per cent) were amazed and delighted to find how much more they earned than they had expected, sometimes twice as much as previously, though two earned less in Community service than before. Pay was considered the decisive factor for about a fifth (21 per cent), but for a slightly higher proportion (23 per cent) considerations of salary did not enter into their calculations. These proportions do confirm that an insufficiently attractive picture was painted of the financial benefits of working for Europe, but they also suggest the weight of considerations other than salary in the decision of whether or not to move to Brussels. Clearly family and personal circumstances were one of those considerations. A high proportion of spouses of the survey group, it emerged, had previous experience of living outside the UK, and often spoke a second language, usually French, which facilitated the move. Ten per cent were bachelors and clearly more mobile than family men. Twenty per cent were divorced or separated at, or soon after, their arrival, a figure which, though there is room for discussion, may lend some support to the theory that for some

53

service in the Community institutions offered or precipitated an escape from unhappy personal circumstances.

Many, indeed the majority, came having burnt their boats back to their previous jobs. Civil servants had return tickets, but of the non-civil servants in the survey group only four had a firm possibility of return if the venture was not a success. Those in the survey group who came feeling they were committed for the rest of their career, usually the older and senior people, who arguably had least to lose, were matched in number almost exactly by those with an open mind and the pragmatic intention to see what it was like and how they got on. Certainly several of the most senior officials from non-civil service backgrounds came with the intention of returning after a few years, confident that they could do so, and regarding their tour as a stint of public service.

Conclusion

The disappointing features of the attempt to recruit Britons to the Community institutions with which we are concerned here resulted largely from a campaign mounted by the Community authorities, with the help of the Civil Service Department, which, while conducted in an unfavourable climate, lacked the dynamism and imagination which might have overcome it. What potential for success it had was undermined by some early mistakes, and unfamiliar and unco-ordinated procedures in Brussels. In common with the other member states new in 1973, the UK authorities had cause to regret the effects of their attention being concentrated too narrowly on the A1-3 levels to the exclusion of all the other grades. In the face of proper Community reluctance to allow the close involvement of the national authorities, however, it is difficult to see that they had an alternative. Though the operation did not at first secure candidates of a consistently high quality in the desired numbers at all levels, both the UK and the Community were fortunate in the end in the talents of many of those finally secured for Brussels. Those who went were, broadly, devoted (to an ideal), different (from their contemporaries at home), discontented (with their lot in the UK), or dutiful (persuaded to go in the public interest). Whatever their specific qualifications and ability, they probably tended to have a wider outlook and experience than the average of their peers at home and, especially when there were no return tickets, exceptional initiative and willingness to face a challenge. Experience was to prove the value of both qualities in the environment into which they moved.

NOTES

(1)   This and subsequent quotations from UK or Community officials derive from interviews given on a non-attributable basis.

(2)   For example, David Spanier, 'Eurocrats wanted', The Times, 21 November 1972.

(3)   For example, The Times, 24 November 1972.

(4)   The Economist, 23 October 1972.

(5)   ibid.

(6)   The Sunday Times, 24 February 1973.

(7)   As a result of experience during the recruitment at the enlargement the system was later changed.

(8)   'Ebauche de profil du fonctionnaire Europeen', Unpublished Commission paper IX A336, 26 April 1972.

(9)   Quoted in Lawrence Scheinmann and Werner Feld, 'The EEC and National Civil Servants of Member States', International Organisation, Winter 1972, Vol. 26, No.1.

(10) For a detailed description of the survey see Appendix I.

III EXPERIENCE IN BRUSSELS

There can be few who went to Brussels confident of success and not many who had any clear idea of what to expect there. The Commission in particular had a somewhat daunting reputation as a place in which to work. It combined the administrative traditions of each of the three original Communities with the differing styles of the Six, and was to have to accommodate those of three more member states, yet it lacked a strong central administration to weld them into coherence. The multinational, multilingual environment was known to make heavy demands on the adaptability and efficiency of staff responsible for performing tasks unusual in their range, importance and potential effects. All Community officials had faced the need to adapt to the difficulties as well as the rewards of the multinational context, and many of the reactions reported by Britons to work in the Community and life in Brussels were common to the majority, whatever their nationality.

Those who came in 1973, however, whether Irish, Danish or British, came into an organisation established without the influence of their particular administrative and cultural traditions, and to an atmosphere somewhat different from that of the heady pioneering and idealistic days of the 1950s and early 1960s, when most of their colleagues had started work there. This, together with their own differing national attitudes and styles of administration, inevitably gave them a different perspective on some aspects of life and work in Community institutions. Like all other officials, the newly arrived Britons had not only the professional but the personal dimension to accommodate. Many had to think about installing and integrating a family into a new way of life as well as learning a new profession in an unusually difficult working environment. This chapter looks at the experience of Britons from the time they arrived in Brussels, as conveyed through interviews with the survey group(1), on both the domestic and professional fronts. The two are considered together not only because they are interdependent but also because of the suggestion that fears of difficulties on the domestic front may have been a deterrent to candidates, and may have contributed to the drop-out rate amongst Britons once recruited.

Getting established in the office

For the majority of Britons it was not a particularly easy start. The lack of co-ordination evident in the Community's handling of the recruitment also made the reception and successful integration of newcomers something of a lottery, so that the inescapable problems of a multiple transition - work, language, housing, lifestyle etc - were not much mitigated by welcome arrangements in Brussels. There was a certain institutional lack of sympathetic and imaginative understanding of the needs of new arrivals as they settled their families, and often a lack of efficient preparation for them at work as well. The Commission and the Council had limited resources, however, and were themselves in the throes of an enormous upheaval coping with the effects of large-scale retirements and radical reorganisations at the same time as receiving a flood of newcomers of three nationalities. There was confusion in varying degrees in most departments for many weeks, with some staff leaving and some arriving. Newly appointed senior officials of only days' standing sometimes found themselves interviewing potential recruits for posts and tasks of which they knew next to nothing. For some, often very early, very late or very senior arrivals, things went smoothly. Brussels Briefing (from the CSD) in hand, and guided by the Commission's own Vade Mecum, they had a friendly and efficient reception from the Personnel Directorate-General, were paid a large salary advance on their day of arrival and, having spent the night in a pre-booked hotel, quickly found a flat to rent through the Commission's Bureau d'Accueil. They were led to an office with a telephone and a file awaiting their attention. The majority were not usually so lucky, however. They frequently found the Bureau d'Accueil's limited resources overwhelmed and no-one with time to deal with them there or in DG IX, the Personnel Directorate-General, so that they did not know where to find their offices, or how to proceed.

The stories of confusion are legion. It was not uncommon, after months of silence, for telegrams from the Personnel Directorate-General to arrive requesting immediate attendance in Brussels, and then for people to arrive to find themselves met in their new departments with blank astonishment and a daunting 'we were not expecting you'. For some there were no offices, no furniture or no telephone when they arrived; for more there were no clearly defined jobs or unexpectedly unsuitable ones. There arose inevitable suspicion that the best jobs had been taken over by existing functionaries and the dross left to newcomers, or even that the need to accommodate a rush of newcomers had led to the establishment of whole new divisions doing non-essential jobs. It was a common experience that people had to make their own jobs, find their own usefulness, carve their own empires. There was a definite premium on initiative. It was, said one, summing up the experience of many, 'a woefully inadequate reception in terms of work efficiency'. The lack of any formal induction course including any explanation of work methods meant that the learning curve tended to be a very long one. There was a useful week's course attended by most newcomers at the College of Europe in Bruges, which was valued in retrospect also as a means of meeting people and making friends (although very often they were fellow countrymen), and which concentrated on the roles of the Community institutions rather than on how to work within them. It was for a number of newcomers a bewildering and confusing start to a new working life.

The most consistently mentioned source of difficulty in the early months was the necessity of working in a foreign language, usually French. Plunged into an unfamiliar environment and grappling with new, often technical subjects in a foreign language was utterly exhausting. The legalistic approach to problems, with papers prefaced by legal preamble and argued at length with Cartesian logic defining what action could be taken on the basis of the legal situation, contrasted with the approach more familiar to Britons, described as pragmatic, of identifying a problem and exploring solutions, and also required considerable adjustment. Language improved with use and much early morning, evening and weekend study. Fonctionnaires of the Six may often be found to pay perhaps somewhat surprised tribute to the level of proficiency achieved by the British. Language was an issue of some importance to the French especially, and it seems probable that the lack of language chauvinism displayed generally by the British did have an effect in smoothing their path, especially at cabinet level.

The British in the survey group pay almost universal tribute to the friendliness of the initial welcome they received on a personal basis from their immediate colleagues in the offices to which they were sent, even though a number of those colleagues might have aspired to some of the jobs they were filling. There had been a certain apprehension amongst incumbents seeing colleagues retired prematurely and not always voluntarily, and faced with the uncertain effects on the established pattern of large numbers of recruits with different approaches and different languages, not least on their own promotion prospects. Any latent resentment which existed was only rarely felt personally by the newcomers, who experienced with gratitude much support and kindliness in the early days, which was extended for the most part into the time, embarrassing for some, of the renegotiation and the referendum.

Getting established outside the office

Outside the office the problems of getting established in the first few months, especially with a family, were many and various. They ranged from the large scale, such as schooling and housing, to the minor but troublesome, such as how to open a joint bank account and where to find good English-speaking doctors and lawyers. The long-established British community in Brussels had not been centred on the Community but as increasing numbers of Britons came to work there with each passing month throughout 1973 this sort of information was increasingly available and exchanged amongst them, with mutual support extended in an atmosphere of universal and undiscriminating comradeliness, reminiscent, in the words of one survivor, of a demobilisation camp. Certainly the British-style pubs near the Berlaymont, the Drum and the Queen Victoria and, later, the Corkscrew, were thronged with new British Community officials exchanging information and making friends. The English-speaking churches of all denominations were major meeting places and sources of support, playing a significant role in helping families to settle. The already established English Comedy Club and the American Theatre Company, the European Choir and local cultural groups, such as the Uccle symphony orchestra, were points of departure into a social life outside work for many. A wide variety of sporting activities, from sailing to squash, from orienteering to golf, though often expensive, provided meeting places for new friendships. Political clubs were soon founded, with former civil servants, hitherto inhibited in such activity, not infrequently emerging as leading lights. For others, international organisations such as the Rotary Clubs or Soroptimists were a source of friendship and support.

It is noticeable, however, how few Britons, in the midst of all this joining, joined the staff associations of the Community; certainly the majority of the survey group did not do so. If the British seemed (and continue to seem) cliquish in associating so much with each other, it is a characteristic shared by other national groups and has much to do with the need to relax from the stress of a totally new environment among compatriots speaking the same language. Aware of the drawbacks of the British appearing as a national block, Sir Christopher Soames's cabinet decided, after his successful and widely appreciated welcome party for British A1-A3s in the summer of 1973, that it was wiser not to repeat the occasion. It was a decision reflecting a scrupulous and proper concern to be, and to be seen to be, sufficiently communautaire, an attitude which in its other manifestations was, however, to contribute to later and unforeseen consequences for the morale of Britons in the Community (see below p.70). Meanwhile, the British in all the Community institutions have joined with other English-speaking expatriates in sustaining a vigorous British cultural life in Brussels. There is a range of activities from Gilbert and Sullivan to madrigals, children's opera and Shakespeare, which in some ways excels that available in British provincial towns and the London suburbs.

Housing was not a particular problem as rented accommodation, at least, was available and the Bureau d'Accueil's list of flats was usually helpful. House purchase was more difficult with high prices, high taxes and Commission funds for cheap mortgages exhausted before enlargement. At the beginning anyway it seemed unwise to many to sell property in the UK to buy in Belgium. Of those interviewed who had rented, as most did at first, the overwhelming majority commented spontaneously and bitterly on their experience of landlords, feeling that they had been 'ripped off' for thousands of francs through the etat de lieu, the fiercely punitive inventory-taking which accompanies the surrender of a lease.

Family considerations
Schooling loomed as a particularly large problem in the early days. The European school, free for fonctionnaires, was run on Continental lines very foreign to the British tradition, and though an English section was set up for the newcomers it was some time before it geared itself to operate in a way satisfactory to British parents. They were alarmed by features ranging from circulars about school activities written exclusively in French (to the confusion of any mothers whose French was minimal) to the lack of extra-curricular activities such as sport, and the frankly poor facilities for teaching science. Confidence in the school increased with the setting up of a second branch in Woluwe (the east Brussels suburb where many expatriates live), and the increasing number of places gained at British universities, including Oxford and

Cambridge. Many of the survey group with children had sent them there for a time at least, or to local Belgian primary schools.

Different problems developed later, however. The Community's system of allowances seemed to some to discriminate unfairly against any British children who were unsuited to the multilingual and highly academic secondary level in the European School, for whom education in the Belgian schools was not a suitable alternative. The British School of Brussels, though it made generous rebates available to the lower paid, cost as much as an English public school, which was the other expensive possibility. It is important to many British families, as it is to officials of other nationalities, that their children should have roots in their country of origin and enjoy at least part of their education there. This often seems most appropriate at the tertiary stage, and here too the structure of Community allowances for children educated elsewhere than at universities seems particularly hard on the British for whom university education even now is not as easily accessible as in many other Community countries. Moreover, British Community officials are being increasingly refused local authority grants for their children's tertiary education in the UK in contrast to the experience of other member state nationals, whose children enjoy rights to such education as if their parents lived in their country of origin. This bears particularly hard, of course, on the junior and lower paid officials of whom there are too few who are British and who need to be encouraged to come to Brussels in greater numbers. Education is perhaps a perennial problem for all expatriates, but many of the survey remarked how glad they were that their children were experiencing the benefits of exposure to different cultures, and learning foreign languages.

There were no arrangements organised by the Community institutions to welcome wives and families and help them settle, such as the multinational companies in Brussels have found it worth setting up for the families of their expatriate employees, though the Belgians generously run a popular 'Welcome to Belgium' programme to show foreigners selected aspects of Belgian life. Undoubtedly many wives found the first year in Brussels particularly difficult. As well as supporting husbands adapting to often difficult conditions in the office and children settling into a new and very different school, wives had to adjust to separation from the familiar, from friends and family at home and sometimes from children at boarding school for the first time, while experiencing an isolation not suffered by the rest of the family, often reinforced by their lack of Flemish and poor French. A few saw, as one interviewee put it, '20 years of housewifely experience going for nothing' as they adjusted to housekeeping in a different environment, grappling with unfamiliar cuts of meat and unidentifiable products on the supermarket shelves. On the other hand, they encountered a range of foodstuffs and a variety of services to delight all but the most unadventurous. Mutual support with other newly arrived wives helped overcome initial difficulties. The churches' activities, language classes, and the increasingly wide range of activities available at the British and Commonwealth Women's Club were contact points for many. The Community's Femmes d'Europe, a charity fund-raising organisation, both benefitted from and benefitted the British wives who joined it, as did the already established Community Help Service, the mental health, counselling and therapeutic centre for the English-speaking community. CHS also ran Help Line, a Samaritan-like emergency telephone answering service which some British Commission and Council wives helped to set up and run.

Employment for wives
The lack of jobs and career opportunities was often mentioned by the survey group as a source of frustration and unhappiness in wives, which grew as the earlier problems of managing a household in a new environment were conquered and the novelty of the new situation wore off. There is certainly a pool of highly qualified and under-used talent amongst British Commission and Council wives. The British and Commonwealth Women's Club is reputed to have conducted a survey which discovered amongst expatriate British wives in Brussels enough unemployed nurses to staff a hospital wing and enough teachers to run an average-sized school. The problem is that employment opportunities in an English-speaking environment are limited and for employment on the open market proficiency in both the Flemish and French languages is often necessary. Again initiative is at a premium and there are many examples of wives who have transferred careers, often in teaching (one founded her own nursery school), or have retrained (one as a solicitor), or have become successful antique dealers, professional writers, musicians or painters.

There is no doubt that the unhappy experience of some homesick wives in Brussels has precipitated decisions to leave Community service or contributed to separations or divorces. This could conceivably be a bigger problem in the Community than in other international organisations. Because of the need to recruit a range of officials at all levels at one time a higher proportion than usual came in middle age and mid-career having previously pursued

62

home-based professions. Their wives and well established families may have been less able and willing to accept radical change than the younger families with less firmly established roots of men recruited at the entry grades. There is a notable contingent of grass widower weekend commuters to the UK. Such problems can, however, be vastly exaggerated. One ex-civil servant interviewed would like to have taken up his return ticket and returned to Whitehall, but said that it was pressure from his wife and family which persuaded him to stay.

Popularity of Brussels

Though for single people Brussels scarcely compares with the glamour of Paris or the bustle of London, almost no-one in our survey actively disliked it as a place to live and most positively enjoyed it. It was described as a good and safe city in which to bring up children, a city of pleasantly manageable size which had come to terms with the motor car and had lots of open green parks and woods. People liked the ease and speed with which they could get to the office, and the ease with which they could travel to other parts of Europe. They liked the range of accessible activities, and the pleasant and varied circle of acquaintances and friends open to them. Several regretted the distance, expense and occasional difficulty of travel to the UK, and individuals missed features of English life such as the public library and 'a decent local newspaper'. A few expressed regret at their feeling of isolation as foreigners from the social, political and community life of the country in which they lived. They would have liked, for example, to have been able to stand for local office elsewhere than on the local Council for Foreigners. There was irritation too at aspects of the local bureaucracy which impinged on daily life. All the grumbles about Brussels as such were minor, however, and were symptomatic of a certain deracine feeling probably inevitable in expatriate life. Indeed, living in Brussels was itself considered an advantage of Community service by many.

Positive aspects of Community service

Financial security and virtual freedom from money worries such as they had experienced in the UK were rated very highly amongst the advantages of working for the Community by almost all those interviewed. The level of remuneration ensured a comfortable life and was a stepping-stone to a wider variety of activities and a fuller life than would probably have been within reach in the UK. It was felt, however, by some, perhaps a little defensively, that income levels were liable to be misunderstood and exaggerated at home. Salaries were not much higher, it was said, than those obtained by friends who were, for example, successful accountants in the UK, and there were no company cars. Salaries were lower than those paid by multinational corporations on the Continent and amounted to much less than the earnings of the international lawyers who sometimes faced Commission lawyers across the Court in Luxembourg. They were a justifiable and necessary recompense for the difficulties of an expatriate life and its effect on the extended family, for the added expenditure it involved, and for the responsibilities and undoubted difficulties of working in a foreign language in a multinational organisation.

Also rated very highly were the rewards of working in an international environment with people of widely differing cultural backgrounds, which interviewees described as 'more stimulating', 'more interesting', 'more fun' than before. It was common for people to cite the positive satisfaction gained from their role, however small, in 'working for Europe', 'the privilege of helping to build Europe', 'getting in on the ground floor of an experiment in multinational and multicultural relations', 'having the chance to work in the centre of a new piece of international machinery', as one of the major advantages of working in the Commission or Council. There was a satisfaction to be derived from the 'prestige of being a Eurocrat', and an undeniable psychological reward 'to anyone possessed of normal human vanity', in finding oneself speaking for the Commission with microphone and earphones, in the 'hot seat' in the Council, or being the Commission's representative while abroad on mission. The opportunity to travel for the Commission, and the possibility of achieving eventually a sought-after post in one of the Commission's information offices or delegations abroad, was also an attractive proposition to one or two of the young A6-7s.

Job satisfaction
Job satisfaction as such is recognised to be extremely variable in the Commission generally. As the Spierenburg Report(2) commented succinctly, 'the Commission is being managed in a manner and with techniques which are inappropriate in present circumstances and which affect morale and efficiency'. Just under half of the survey group rated job satisfaction as one of the positive aspects of their working life in the Commission. The degree of job satisfaction did not seem to depend on rank, though one A3 asserted that it was 'at this level that things begin to get interesting', nor upon previous background or experience. One Director-General found his job satisfaction much lower than he had had in Whitehall 'despite the greater challenge and potential'

because of 'a lower level of administrative competence', and a young ex-civil servant at A7 agreed that after so rigorous an entrance examination he was disappointed to come to a job much less demanding than the one he had held previously. Yet others even with similar civil service backgrounds, and ranks between A2 and A4, described their job satisfaction as 'much more than in the past', 'immense', and commented 'the work is fully absorbing, varied, hard and satisfying', or 'the work is more varied and stimulating and has a higher intellectual content'. Those from non-civil service backgrounds who agreed, and who had made the double step from private industry to international civil service, remarked on the attraction for them of the element of public service in their work - 'the sense of doing something worthwhile', 'the sense of being close to the centre of things', 'where the action is'.

The main variable in job satisfaction, whatever the rank, was the area in which the interviewee worked. Areas where the Commission has real power under the Treaties, as in DG VI (Agriculture), or DG IV (Competition), or DG I (External Relations), and policy areas in the political limelight of concern to active Commissioners and member states, were more rewarding than the service areas such as the Personnel Department DG IX, Financial control DG XX, and the non-policy levels in DG XIX, the Department of the Budget. One official who declared he had 'fantastic' job satisfaction had worked with and for those with greatest real power in DG VI and the Secretariat-General on issues of current importance to the Community.

In other departments such satisfaction can be harder to come by. In non-policy areas a lack of impetus, the effects of the endemic maldistribution of staff, insufficient devolution of responsibility, and the narrow, routine nature of some of the tasks, were considerations which led to some officials, most often at A4-5, feeling insufficiently employed, under-used and bored. A few, usually older officials were reconciling themselves to a less than challenging time at work, complementing it by an active life outside and considering the option of an early retirement. It is striking, however, how many of those who enjoyed their jobs commented that they had had to go out to make their jobs interesting; 'someone more diffident would have had a hard job to integrate and would have got boring work'; 'things do not come to you, you have to look for interesting areas, seek them out even when your job seems defined'; 'the place is so structured much of the interest is up for grabs', and finally 'here you make your own work, you have to be a self-starter - if you only do the work dumped on your desk you will not have enough to do'.

Reservations

One source of frustration widely commented upon at all levels was the way in which months or years of dedicated work could be summarily set aside by the refusal of the Council of Ministers to adopt a proposal. The measure of this frustration, one interviewee suggested, could be gauged by the annual document produced by the Council Secretariat on decisions pending, in 1980 some 150 pages with an average of four decisions per page, each 'postponed' decision representing the disappointment of the department and individuals who drafted it and worked upon it. They represent the counterpart, the reverse side, of the satisfaction engendered by successfully 'building Europe', the results, in the words of a Director-General, 'of the unwillingness of member states at the political level to pool national interests for the common good reflected in the lack of will towards change in the Council of Ministers'. The role of the Commissioners' cabinets in suppressing, rejecting without consultation, or otherwise interfering with the work of directorates-general, often when it was far advanced, was also recorded as a source of perennial irritation and frustration, especially by the senior grades who most often had the ground cut from under their feet. The cabinets were bitterly described as 'inexpert people who switch in at the last moment and disturb a careful edifice', or, put more directly, 'the cabinets represent an extra layer of ignorant interference'. These problems are common to all nationalities, however, and had no particular dimension peculiar to Britons in the Commission. Spierenburg,(3) for example, commented on both 'the failure of the Council to adopt proposals which have required months of hard work to prepare' and the 'lack of structural co-ordination among directorates-general and a growing emphasis on the roles of the personal staffs of Commissioners' (the cabinets) as factors tending to lower morale.

Another drawback to Commission service constantly mentioned by Britons and shared by all the member state nationals was career expectation, and the difficulties in achieving advancement or a change of job. Promotion was not necessarily regarded, as some Britons pointed out, as desirable for additional income or added job interest, but rather for 'increased status in a status-conscious environment'. The way that Community staff have been recruited, in waves, has resulted in an undesirable age distribution so that in the normal course of things the few retirements expected up to 1986, the low turnover of staff, and the reluctance of the Council to authorise new posts, have created serious bottlenecks and made promotion rates generally slow. The elements of political and 'geographical' balance in promotions to A3 and above have meant that, though most people could expect eventually to make it to A4, above that level promotion was chancy, 'Your face has to fit', said one Briton. From A7 to A4 promotion was dependent on an accumulation of points for age, length of service, and performance together with the Director-General's recommendation, which even below A3 was itself, in the opinion of many, sometimes too dependent on considerations of nationality and patronage. Some of those interviewed felt that officials from the new member states had been discriminated against by the points system, because, until the system was changed (largely as a result of pressure from new member state governments), only experience gained inside the house, and not relevant experience gained previously, counted towards promotion, with consequent disadvantage to lately arrived newcomers. Others suggested that perhaps the promotion rate for Britons was justifiably slow, because some had been given some-what senior gradings at a young age upon joining. Promotion opportunities were unfairly distributed, it was felt (and the Commission would agree), with the greater number of opportunities in expanding areas perhaps not readily available to good people beavering away diligently and competently in areas outside the limelight.

The British thus share with other nationalities the deterrent effect on the young, able and ambitious, of the long service requirements for promotion and the elements of chance in whether the A3 barrier is broken. The two Britons with the most outstanding record of promotions both left the Commission after two promotions but before they had completed nine years service, and though other factors came into their decisions to leave both had been daunted by the prospect of a long wait for a further promotion, and the A3 hurdle. Both had otherwise thoroughly enjoyed their work, and one did not exclude the possibility of a return to the Commission in later years, perhaps as a national nominee for a senior post. Some other able and ambitious A6s and A5s interviewed were similarly discouraged and poised to leave. Perspectives on this issue could change, however, with the improvement of promotion prospects when the wave of retirements comes in 1985, and if the Spierenburg proposals to enhance the prospects of insiders reaching the senior positions were ever to be implemented.

Similarly proposals to facilitate mobility within the Commission were endorsed by Britons interviewed. In the absence of a strong central personnel department planning careers, and with the emphasis on specialists beavering away at their own specialism

67

rather than on generalists specialising in the art of administration and tackling problems in a variety of spheres in the tradition of the British Civil Service, mobility between jobs and departments in the Commission tends to be limited. Some Britons interviewed regretted the limitations the lack of mobility placed on their career prospects in general and their chances of widening their experience. More explicity, those in unsatisfactory jobs regretted that their chances of leaving them were restricted. Opportunities to move were rare and difficult to achieve, and could, where there was no system of centralised job assessment and an unreliable system of confidential reports, delay promotion. It was a situation the Commission was working to change, and once again the Spierenburg Report diagnosed this complaint as a general malaise. 'The limited scope of many officers' work and their excessive specialisation, their lack of information about Commission policy in general and especially the feeling that they are too remote from the decision makers, all act as disincentives'(4). Comments on the effect of this lack of information on the overall policy of the Commission were also endorsed by interviewees, two of whom were led by the extent of their frustration to suggest, however unconstitutionally, that there was a role for national Representations to play in filling the gap.

British traditions of administration were reflected in the reservations Britons in the survey group generally reported when faced with aspects of the Commission's internal work practices. The formality and rigidity of the hierarchy attracted widespread unfavourable comment. Though there could be a high level of informal responsibility, there was little delegation of formal responsibility, to the extent that even permission to take leave or the signing of letters leaving the directorate-general were dealt with in some departments exclusively at the highest level. The formality of the convention, stronger in some departments than others, whereby a junior was discouraged from approaching a head of department direct without going through the intermediate ranks, and where contacts with other departments should be made only at the appropriate parallel rank, was felt to be irksome and inefficient. The more informal approach of the new member state nationals, however, was thought to be having an effect in eroding that convention. The similarly formal and inflexible system of authorising expenditure was described as over bureaucratic (with, for example, 60 signatures necessary to send an expert to Singapore) and as ineffective and cramping of initiative.

The practice, derived from French methods of administration, of not keeping central working files may have had the advantage of stimulating new approaches to a subject but it confounded the British, especially the ex-civil servants. An ill-informed approach was often deemed the more likely result, especially when combined with the excessive compartmentalisation within the Commission, and the general lack of consultation and widespread reluctance to share information. These themselves were born out of an individualistic approach foreign to Britons reared on traditions of teamwork, and were fostered by the lack of security afforded to the individual by the weak central management structures. The high ratio of officials to support staff meant that highly paid officials of all nationalities could spend an unjustifiable proportion of their time organising the typing and translation, photocopying and circulation of their work (a phenomenon, however, not perhaps unknown in national administrations). The shortage of adequate numbers of English-speaking secretaries and their erratic distribution between departments was felt to be a special burden for British officials. Moreover, the poor staff discipline, one of the results of the weak central management, seemed to be regarded by the British as especially pernicious. At A3 and above the difficulties of insisting on good time-keeping and responsible work performance, when effective sanctions are difficult to enforce because of cumbersome procedures laid down in the staff regulations, were a common subject of comment and regret. More than one A3 said he could endorse the forthright remarks on the subject by Sir Roy Denman, Director-General of DG I who had advocated trenchantly and controversially that dismissal of unsatisfactory staff should be made easier in the interests of internal discipline.(5)

Areas of difference

Where the majority of the Britons felt they differed most from their Community colleagues was in their reaction to, and slow realisation of, how far, in the absence of a strong central administration, their career pattern and their advancement depended on their own initiative. Career management in the Commission was, they found, up to the individual to an extent unusual to most Britons, especially if they came from a civil service or other institutional background. It involved a degree of self-promotion and patronage alien to usual British administrative practice with which few felt comfortable, and which put them at a disadvantage at first among colleagues not reared on Northcote/Trevelyan precepts(6) and from bureaucracies where patronage, political and personal, was not uncommon. They felt further handicapped in this context by the quality and quantity of support they received inside the Commission from the cabinets of the British Commissioners, and from the British Government through the UK's Permanent Representation.

Role of cabinets

There was a widespread feeling amongst the survey group that, whereas the other nationalities had officials in the cabinets or in the Representations prepared to work actively to promote the interests of their nationals within the Commission, throwing their influence behind attempts to gain promotion or transfer to jobs of greater interest, the corresponding British officials had taken a high-minded and idealistic attitude to such matters. This was felt to have been inappropriate, in view of existing practice in the Commission, and to have resulted in individual Britons being disadvantaged in competition for promotion and the national interest being ill-served as British candidates were not apparently supported to fill vacancies of obvious potential importance to the UK. Some nationalities, it was felt, were at one extreme pulling every available string to such an extent that it was counter-productive. There was the story of the Italian huissier (messenger) who had mustered letters from two Cabinet Ministers to support his interests, for instance. While it was recognised, however, that there was some productive virtue in being seen to be fair, the British were generally felt to have gone to the other extreme and behaved with so disinterested a rectitude as to invite the charge of naivety.

Cabinet interference in appointment procedures, 'with undue weight being given to nationality factors',(7) was a practice acknowledged and condemned. The early British cabinets had seen the extent and harmful effect of the system of lobbying for jobs and promotion where, in the absence of appropriate personnel management tools, the noisy rather than the good candidate was likely to be preferred. They decided at the end of 1973 to try to bring influence to bear in an attempt to denationalise and depoliticise promotions and appointments below A3. At A1-3 where consideration of nationality factors was recognised as legitimate, they were determined to operate as hard and as ruthlessly as anyone else, but at A4-7 they did aim to get cabinets out of the field, to function not as national staffing shops but as rubber stamps to director-generals' recommendations. Partly as a result of those British efforts cabinets are now supposed to be excluded from promotions up to A4. However, the most striking and longest lasting result of that early decision seems to have been that many British A4-7 were left with the unfortunate impression

70

that they could not muster patronage and support in influential quarters in the same way as their Community colleagues.

With the change of Commissioners and portfolios in 1977, that impression seems to have been reinforced. A Briton, Roy Jenkins, became the President of the Commission, and the junior British Commissioner, Christopher Tugendhat, was given responsibility for Personnel and Administration. Both British Commissioners not unreasonably felt a particular need to be seen to be above reproach in handling their respective management responsibilities. Attempts to introduce measures of reform into personnel procedures based on disinterested fairness dictated even greater scrupulousness. Cabinet officials affirm nevertheless that advice, and occasionally active help, was systematically extended to all who asked for it, and information collected on British 'A' grade officials so that recommendations could be made when required. All too often, however, it was believed that in leaning over backwards to make sure that the highest standards of disinterest-edness were maintained and the British Commissioners were not seen to use the influence of their portfolios to favour Britons unduly, their nationals were actually handicapped and disadvan-taged. The comment of a non-British observer in a German Commissioner's cabinet, that the British are more discreet in any patronage extended, and therefore more effective, may hold the truth of the matter, but if so, discretion has exacted a price in terms of morale amongst Britons. At the same time there is, however, a very real possibility that the degree of support given to other member state nationals is overestimated. 'We are all,' said the same official, 'rather the victims of the French will-of-steel, eagle-eyed, purposeful placement myth.'

While regretting their apparent lack of support, many Britons in the survey group expressed their extreme distaste at the need to lobby on their own behalf and their reluctance to do so. They would find it hard, some said, to bring themselves and their aspirations to the notice of the cabinets or the Permanent Representation. Most Britons, it was agreed, had a certain cultural block about having to push themselves forward, which was itself a handicap, yet in the Commission a supine confidence that merit would bring its own reward was likely to be misplaced. Some had come to terms realistically with the necessity for the individual to mobilise his own support, and a few even gave every appearance of doing it with skill and gusto, like the man reported to have mustered a letter from a British Prime Minister and the Irish President to support his cause. For a majority, however, the

71

apparent need for support, their own reluctance to seek it and the perceived difficulty of obtaining it, combined to produce a special British grievance with implications of some seriousness for morale and effectivenss.

Role of national authorities

At another level British Community officials expressed their concern at the apparent inactivity on the part of the government on the question of British under-representation. The apparent lack of interest shown by the authorities in helping British nationals into vacant posts of obvious interest such as in the Fisheries Directorate-General, the Regional Fund, or the Social Fund, was perplexing. British officials contrasted what they saw as long-term strategic planning in a campaign to capture useful posts waged by some member states with Britain's seemingly haphazard approach. So intense was the concern that more than one took to compiling statistics and case histories to stimulate action from the national authorities. It was very possible that some individuals over-estimated the powers of any government to interfere in the internal affairs of what was after all an independent organisation. There were others who took the sternly communautaire view that national governments had no legitimate role to play in Community affairs below a certain level anyway. The contrasting attitudes posed the dilemma of the UK government authorities. The fact, however, that there was such widespread ignorance of the changing attitude of the British Government (which we shall trace in the next chapter) and its increasing concern over numbers, distribution and the morale of Britons, was itself symptomatic of the lack of contact and poor communication between British officials, especially those below A3 and in low profile departments, and government representatives. Though contact with senior officials in key areas was recognised to be assiduously maintained, it was felt among the survey group that insufficient care and attention was given to fostering contact between the Representation and British officials at the rank and file level, to their mutual disadvantage.

There was a feeling too, on the one hand that ex-civil servants were privileged in this regard because of their connections in Whitehall, and on the other, that amongst Britons in the Commission the ex-civil servants especially were regarded in some way as renegades, who were now beyond the pale. Such feelings were sometimes inadvertently encouraged by departments in Whitehall. One quite senior civil servant of over twenty-five years' standing was mortified when he gave up his return ticket to receive only a cyclostyled form letter terminating his connection with his department, together with a refusal to extend to him the privilege of continued receipt of the departmental internal newsletter. Episodes such as the neglect of the position of Britons in the Community institutions in the British Nationality Bill, which it took a vigorous campaign and powerful representations to get amended, and situations such as the disenfranchisement of Britons in the institutions in both British and European parliamentary elections, combined to reinforce the feeling that British officials generally, and their legitimate interests, were not sufficiently considered.

The Council Secretariat

Though they shared some of the views of their colleagues in the Commission about the practical difficulties of the multinational dimension, Britons in the Council Secretariat seemed to have a higher degree of job satisfaction, and in a smaller close-knit organisation in constant communication with Permanent Representations, none of their feelings of neglect. Morale in the 'back room' jobs seemed comparably lower, but in general, because they were in the centre of affairs and playing the 'honest broker role' of guiding matters through the network of Committees and Councils rather than hatching ideas and negotiating their acceptance, like the Commission, the Council staff were better placed to see faster results, and morale benefitted. British promotion rates at A3 and above had been very adequate, aided perhaps by some early departures of senior Britons returning to the foreign service, and there were no complaints at any level that Britons felt disadvantaged compared with their colleagues of other nationalities. There was, however, regret at the lower levels about promotion prospects, job mobility and the lack of a conventional personnel system, and also concern at the under-representation of Britons on the staff. One A6, who had enjoyed a stimulating if sometimes overworked stint in the Council, had come to the view that it was wisest for an ambitious young man to regard the Community as a useful and fascinating place to spend a number of years before moving on.

Those who left

It seems probable that the difficulties of working successfully in a multinational environment far outweigh any difficulties in family adjustments as a likely cause of Britons leaving the service of the Community. Seven of the twenty-four Britons who left permanent service in the 'A' grades between 1977 and the summer of 1980 were interviewed, and for only one were family difficulties a factor. For the others the elements of frustration they had encountered in their work were more compelling reasons for declining to stay on in Brussels. These included the difficulties well known to the Commission and mentioned in interviews by the survey group: lack of promotion prospects, alien work methods, talent not always used effectively with resulting lack of job satisfaction, less than skilful staff management and too evident an emphasis on nationality. Britons who resigned tended to return to the areas which they had left to come to the Community, like the senior officials who left after three or four years to return to the City, industry, banking or the Civil Service. Others went into areas as diverse as the Church, War on Want, Shell and the World Bank. Four went into academic life (one to the London Business School). It seems, and Community and Council officials concur in this, that experience in the Community is considered an advantage in seeking jobs outside only if professional skills and technical expertise are kept up to date. Employability seems likely to decline after too long spent in Brussels unless an official has been successful in a high profile, active area of Community competence where expertise is marketable. Thus a young man with just such experience in DG VI (Agriculture) left the Commission for a very senior job dealing with the marketing of dairy products. Another obviously likely source of employment is the interest groups centred on the Community, such as the European Consumers' Bureau to which an official from the Council migrated. Otherwise it is not obvious that experience in Community institutions as such is tempting to employers, or even, as we shall see, to the Civil Service, while the difficulty of obtaining comparable salaries outside is a notable inhibition to those who might otherwise think of leaving.

Conclusion

The year of the first enlargement was easy neither for the old nor the new staff of the Community institutions. The newcomers had much to learn, and though most settled successfully in Brussels, speedy integration into their new working environment was not facilitated by the somewhat haphazard working of the reception arrangements. From the account of Britons working in the Commission a picture emerges of an unfamiliar, challenging and often difficult environment, where the potential for frustration is greater than usually encountered but where the real and psychological rewards can be high enough to outweigh this. They found that jobs can vary enormously in their scope and value, but that an able, enterprising and adaptable person can build a career exceptional in its importance, influence and satisfaction. Difficulties encountered were most often those to which officials of every nationality were subject, and of which the Commission was aware and which it was attempting to remedy. They resulted chiefly from the distinctive and multinational character of the organisation. Since the Commission is unique amongst international organisations and indeed amongst bureaucracies, orthodox civil service models, reflected in the expectations of some of those coming to serve there, were not in the end applicable. Thus, and partly because of their particular cultural values and administrative traditions, many Britons on an individual level have been slow to realise the degree to which job and promotion prospects depend on their own efforts at managing their careers. At the same time, they have felt insufficiently supported in those efforts by the national representatives in the cabinets or in the Permanent Representation by comparison with colleagues from other member states. Where work methods are alien, the influence of the new member states is adapting them a little, and where there are sources of discontent peculiar to the British, they are increasingly being tackled. We look at the progress of both in the next chapter.

NOTES

(1)   For details of the survey see Appendix I.
(2)   Proposals for Reform of the Commission of the European Communities and its Services. Report by an independent Review Body under the Chairmanship of Mr Dirk Spierenburg. EEC Publication, 1979, p.16, para.4.
(3)   ibid. p.6. para.21 and p.5 para. 18.
(4)   ibid. p.6 para. 21.
(5)   Reported in The Times, 14 April 1980.
(6)   Report on the Organisation of the Permanent Civil Service, 1854. Reprinted in the Fulton Report, The Civil Service, 1968. HMSO Cmnd. 3638.
(7)   Spierenburg report, op.cit. p.19 para. 56.

IV WHITEHALL

If in Brussels there were cultural factors which delayed and hindered the complete and comfortable integration of Britons into the Community institutions, there can be few doubts that the prevarications and doubts of the renegotiation and the referendum, and subsequently the negative attitudes of some Ministers towards Community membership, delayed the pace of Whitehall's adaptation to the need to 'think European'. More specifically, the stumble at the start of British participation in the institutions delayed getting to grips with problems of Community staffing and obstructed the process of mutual accommodation and familiarisation between Whitehall and Brussels. Though by the end of the decade of her accession the UK had developed seemingly satisfactory machinery and methods to deal with differing aspects of Community staffing, some problems might never have arisen in the form or to the extent that they did had there not been the period of uncertainty and near disengagement so soon after entry.

At the end of the recruitment period the CSD had retained central responsibility for Whitehall's interest in Community staffing, sending officials from time to time to Brussels to talk to compatriots in the institutions about any problems within their sphere, such as return-ticket arrangements. The potential problems inherent in the numbers and the variable quality of the British contingent had been noted in the Cabinet Office very soon after accession. Early remedial action was precluded, however, by the process of renegotiation and the referendum, during which Community staffing was relegated to a low priority. Numbers of British candidates presenting themselves for advertised vacancies at all levels declined abruptly and even the two-week familiarisation courses in Brussels run for civil servants fell from being heavily oversubscribed to being barely filled. Reawakening interest was accelerated in 1977-78 with the return from Brussels

76

of a senior civil servant to be the Deputy Secretary in charge of
European co-ordination in the Cabinet Office. Familiar with the
British situation in Brussels and aware of its implications
prejudicial to the national and Community interest, he was
instrumental in securing a change of gear on the issue and bringing
it to the attention of the highest official and ministerial levels. It
was agreed that the need to improve numbers and quality was such
that it required a political initiative to try to secure preferential
treatment for British candidates. In the same way as the Dutch
Government repeatedly drew attention at a high level to the
problem of Dutch under-representation and asked for special
measures to be adopted to recruit Dutch nationals, the British
embarked on a series of high-level representations drawing
attention to the dimensions of the British problem for the
Community. The Foreign Secretary wrote to the President of the
Commission in April 1978 suggesting a measure of positive discrimination until the field of candidates eligible for potential promotion
was enlarged to a size comparable to that of the other major
states, a line which was pursued by the Prime Minister in meetings
with the President, by ministers of the succeeding government, and
by successive ambassadors to the EEC. The Commission's attitude,
however, was that no such positive discrimination was possible.

Machinery in London
Meanwhile in Whitehall a new Cabinet Office Committee was set
up which took a wide-ranging interest in all aspects of Community
staffing. It was chaired from the European secretariat and
attended by officials from government departments interested in
posts as well as the CSD (later the Management and Personnel
Office), the European Community Department of the FCO, the UK
Permanent Representation in Brussels, and, in the early days, a
representative from the cabinets of the British Commissioners. A
principal task of the Committee was to monitor likely vacancies
and reorganisation proposals affecting staffing, relying primarily
on information from the Permanent Representation. It decided on
an ad hoc basis which posts were to be priority targets at which to
aim British candidates, calculating that long-term strategic
planning was impracticable in view of the limited resources available and the difficulty of making accurate predictions about
changing priorities and changing staffing patterns. Its policy was
to present only candidates of the highest quality, with the best
chance of being selected on merit for the posts for which they
were being put forward. Suitable candidates were to be selected
either from inside the Commission with the help of the UK
Representation, or, where no internal candidate seemed likely to

succeed, from outside it, with the CSD identifying likely candidates from the Civil Service or elsewhere.

Such an arrangement, whereby suitable candidates are identified by circulating Civil Service departments and organisations and people outside the Civil Service known to them, has been criticised as too narrow(1). It can favour recruits from within the Civil Service who are most easily accessible to the Management and Personnel Office and whose suitability is most easily verified by known, i.e. civil service, criteria, and restricts the range of non-civil servants eligible for consideration. Certainly there exist likely and perhaps suitable candidates who will not be reached by present arrangements and who have a right to be considered. Indeed, there may be some amongst them who might prove of greater service to the Community and the UK than the current range of potential candidates. The Management and Personnel Office are aware of the point and do make conscious efforts to keep the process outward-looking and open to non-civil servants, even though, in the A1-3 posts chiefly in question, the bureaucratic skills and political sensitivity developed in civil servants are of proven usefulness. Whatever the provenance of the officially backed candidates once identified, the Committee recommends appropriate support for them, depending on the level of post either through the UK Representation at Director-General or Director level, or through the British cabinets, or even through ministerial representations to Commissioners, who are responsible ultimately for making the appointment.

The department in the CSD responsible for Community staffing was itself strengthened with the secondment of an additional and experienced Principal. The additional post did not last long in the climate of civil service cut-backs, but the department carried out a number of improvements. A better targeting of circulars about vacancies of all types to likely specialist classes and departments achieved results. Considerable efforts were expended on such matters as bringing the conditions under which civil servants went to Brussels in line with those of other member states, with return-ticket arrangements being extended and tidied up. Ministers endorsed the importance of staffing the Community institutions; Establishment Officers were again reminded of the European dimension and the value to their own departments of sending the best possible people to Brussels. Similarly measures were taken to try to ensure that Permanent Secretaries recognised service in the Communities as valuable and that their departments rewarded it. By such means it was hoped that recalcitrant opinion within the

Civil Service at all levels, but especially in the upper ranks, would be influenced towards a more positive attitude towards serving in the Community than had been current in the early and mid-1970s.

Improved communications

At the same time steps were taken to try to improve communications with existing British _fonctionnaires_, and to develop the British Government's 'pastoral care' of its nationals in the Commission in so far as was consistent with their status as employees of an independent and multinational organisation. When the British Commissioners were no longer operating under the constraints imposed by the Office of President or the Personnel portfolio, staff seconded to their cabinets from Whitehall were briefed on the extent and nature of British under-representation; on the particular problems encountered by Britons in Community institutions; and the effect on morale of the sense most had had of being insufficiently supported. A not uncontroversial initiative was taken by the Permanent Representation to tackle this problem at source in late 1980 by inviting representatives of Britons in the Community institutions in Brussels to a meeting with senior officials from Whitehall. The concerned British approach to the problem of national imbalances and what the authorities were trying to do about them at policy as well as individual level were explained, together with the constraints on what could be achieved. It was stressed that officials as employees of an independent organisation were responsible for being active in their own cause, though the Permanent Representation was available for consultation in cases of difficulty. A frank and free exchange left no doubts as to the degree of frustration felt by some at a whole range of problems, but especially at what they felt had been their disadvantage heretofore in an environment where influence-mongering was believed to be the norm. So useful and therapeutic was the exchange felt to be that it was decided to hold similar meetings regularly to which cabinet officials and representatives of DG IX were invited. To try to minimise future problems of contact and communication it was hoped to set up a system putting all British newcomers in the A grades in touch with the cabinets and the Representation on arrival, and to brief applicants for Community posts on the role of their national authorities even before their arrival.

Roulement

The impetus given to improve the British staffing position by a civil servant returning to Whitehall from the Commission is a striking example of the potential benefits accruing to both the

Community and Whitehall from roulement, the to-ing and fro-ing of officials between Community and national administrations. On the whole, however, the mutual familiarisation and cross-fertilisation of ideas and methods have not occurred with the frequency hoped for in the days before accession. Though some civil servants have taken advantage of their return tickets, the number is comparatively small (central records have not been kept), and there has been no great two-way flow of officials as once envisaged between Brussels and London. On the one hand, many civil servants established as fonctionnaires in Brussels were reluctant to return spontaneously because they enjoyed the wider horizons and greater challenges they found there or were loth to suffer the considerable material sacrifices which a return to the UK would entail, or both; and it is almost unknown for anyone to be invited back to do a specific job, with appropriate incentives. On the other hand, the Civil Service attitudes which had affected the recruitment of 1972-3 were slow to change, apart from a more widespread appreciation of the financial rewards in Brussels.

It was rarely demonstrable to the able and ambitious that service in the Commission actually enhanced career or even immediate job prospects on return to Whitehall, and quite often the reverse seemed to be true. Promotion in absentia was possible but infrequent and occurred chiefly in departments such as the Ministry of Agriculture and the FCO where experience in Brussels was of direct relevance. Attitudes towards promoting people on or soon after their return were generally doubtful; partly because some individuals had been promoted to go to Brussels, and it was felt that they could not return to another promotion without having served in Whitehall at the intervening rank. The official view was that 'time spent doing one thing was time not spent doing another', reflecting a perception that the work done in the Commission, for example, was not necessarily relevant to the Civil Service. With no reliable system of confidential reporting on jobs and performance, it was felt that, in a situation where promotion was increasingly difficult at home, it was unjust to the majority to give a prodigal, whether returning from the Community or elsewhere, an advantage over his peers whose jobs and performance had been so monitored. In more than one case a decision not to return to Whitehall has been influenced by the refusal to give bankable assurances about early promotion - assurances which are seldom given to anyone at any time. Some of the considerations involved are changing, however, and it is firmly put about now that it is an advantage to have spent five years in Brussels. But with examples of advantage as yet few and far between, there is still a reluctance amongst the younger civil servants to go to Brussels in large numbers as established officials and difficulty even persists in getting a range of highly qualified candidates for the good jobs at A1-3 when they appear.

Temporary appointments
More numerous and probably more effective as a means of bringing first-hand experience of the Commission back into the body of Whitehall are those who go to Brussels on temporary contracts as agents temporaires. There are at present some 150 agents temporaires of all nationalities in the Commission and some 43 in the Council. They include the officials seconded to the cabinets on a temporary basis, and amongst them it is possible to point to a record of accelerated careers with promotions in absentia and Community expertise put to direct use after return from Brussels. This may owe something to the greater visibility and the obviously demanding nature of cabinet jobs, but it is also true that it is usually the most able and promising officials who are seconded to these jobs anyway, 'flyers' whose careers would be likely to be successful with or without the Brussels dimension. There are as yet few, less than half a dozen, with cabinet experience who have returned to London and the Civil Service. British ex-cabinet members, like their colleagues from other countries, have not been immune from the temptation to 'parachute' into permanent service in the Commission and have sometimes been encouraged to do so by Whitehall as a good means of getting permanent posts filled.

Also classed in practice as agents temporaires are the experts from national administrations who go to the Commission usually for between three months and two years under arrangements made precisely to develop better relationships between the Commission and public administrations. The British now send more experts than other member states(2) (see Table 4.1), perhaps reflecting a need in the Commission for advice on practices and traditions as yet so different from those of the rest of Europe. There is also an exchange scheme set up in 1976 which the British are using intensively (see Table 4.2). According to the Commission, the greatest number of the officials exchanged (five) have gone to DG V (Social Affairs) where the work on the Social Fund was of particular interest, three each to DG I (External Relations) and the Environmental Agency, two each to DG IV (Competition), DG XIII (Energy) and the Customs Union, and one each to DG IX (Personnel), DG VIII (Development), and DG XVIII (Credit and Investments). British officials who go to Brussels under these schemes tend to be single and to be at Higher Executive Officer

Table 4.1　Experts sent to the Commission from Member States: 1979 and 1980

	1979	1980 (up to 30/9/80)
Belgium	12	10
Denmark	2	1
France	17	15
Germany	18	9
Ireland	15	10
Italy	17	11
Luxembourg	-	-
Netherlands	5	3
United Kingdom	31	29

Source:　Answer to written question No.1112/80 (7 November 1980) by Mr Newton Dunn, in the European Parliament.

Table 4.2　Exchanges of Officials between the Commission and Member States: 1979-1981

Member State	1977	1978	1979	1980	1981	Total	Av. duration in months
Belgium	-	-	-	-	1	1	6
Denmark	-	1	1	2	1	2	24
France	1	2	6	7	7	15	10.7
Germany*	4	8	14	23	13	40	8.3
Ireland	3	2	1	-	-	4	9.2
Italy	-	2	3	-	2	7	8.1
Luxembourg	-	-	-	1	-	1	3
Netherlands	2	2	-	2	2	8	13.1
United Kingdom	4	10	10	11	9	20	17.3

Source:　Response given in a Written Question (No.1112/80, Mr Newton Dunn) updated by the Commission in December 1981.

*　Many of the German candidates are fulfilling their obligation to serve in an embassy or international organisation at a certain stage in their career, and usually spend less than 6 months in the Commission.

(A) or Principal level and they come most frequently from Customs and Excise, the Ministry of Agriculture, Fisheries and Food, the Departments of the Environment, Employment and Industry, and the nationalised industries.

The home departments are said to be increasingly recognising the benefits brought by returning agents temporaires and find it worth continuing to send them even when cuts in manpower have made it more difficult to do so. The traffic is largely one way, however, as Commission officials rarely avail themselves of the opportunity to go to national administrations, probably because people were not in the past encouraged to do so because of short staffing in the Commission; DG IX is now trying to encourage an outward flow, however. While the confidential report factor does still worry departments in Whitehall, it does not seem to have counted against returned agents temporaires, who are away for a shorter period usually in jobs of known relevance to their home departments and who are said to find themselves marked out for fast promotion perhaps in the same way as cabinet staff. Again, there is a tendency amongst them to seek to find ways of staying on in Brussels rather than returning to London. There are other temporary 'Britons in Brussels' from Whitehall but they work not for the Community but for the British Government in the UK Representation to the EC and are outside the scope of this study.

Those who return bring with them understanding of how the Commission really works, a familiarity with other methods and other assumptions in their field of expertise with which to leaven the received views in Whitehall. They help achieve a better informed, more sensitive and so more successful handling of Community affairs. Perhaps of most immediate practical use, they bring to their departments a wide range of professional contacts in the Commission and in the national administrations of other member states. They are also said sometimes to have developed a certain toughness of manner in meetings, born of working in an organisation with fewer gentlemanly conventions and a greater premium on personality.

Though attitudes are changing, participation in Community decision-making has not yet spread extensively enough throughout the Civil Service to have eradicated deep-seated attitudes based on unfamiliarity and national chauvinism, especially in those departments least concerned with Brussels. There the EC still tends to be regarded as an international organisation beyond our shores, foreign, akin to the OECD or the UN rather than to a semidomestic partner in government in a continuing and continuous relationship. It may be symptomatic, for example, that matters arising from UK membership of the Community, including the European Social Fund, are dealt with by the 'Overseas Division of the Department of Employment. The attitude of the British government departments, in common with those of the Danes (but not so much the Irish) contrasts markedly with that of the French or to a lesser extent the Germans, who see a closer identity between the Community and their countries, between its methods and their own. This is often reflected in the greater openness of their national officials to Community officials, a willingness to share documents as well as ideas and information in frequent telephone calls. Several Britons have been struck by the not untypical example of the contrast between the close and frequent contact between the statisticians and economists in DG II, the Economic and Financial Affairs Directorate-General, of the Commission and the French finance and economic ministries,(3) and the much more distant relationship that exists between that DG and the UK Treasury. Many factors have contributed to such contrasts, and though perhaps quite such a degree of easy intimacy will be hard to achieve, time and increasing first-hand experience of working in the Commission transported back to Whitehall may lessen them. Meanwhile there has been the suggestion in the Spierenburg Report that there should be provision for some 200 short-contract posts at A4-5 in the Commission to be filled chiefly by officials from national administrations or public enterprises, made partly so that 'the Commission will benefit from the more informed view of its activities which they will take back to their home administrations'(4). It demonstrates the value the Commission places on spreading first-hand experience of its working amongst national civil servants, which could only prove helpful if it should come to pass and if the British authorities took full advantage of the opportunities it provided.

Comparative mutual influence of Brussels and Whitehall

Before the UK joined the Community it had been suggested that membership might affect some of the traditional values of the Civil Service. The anonymity and political impartiality of civil servants, the Service's independence from political influence and 'objective' standards in recruitment and promotion, as well as the lack of specialist qualifications amongst general administrators and the tradition of the 'gifted amateur', might undergo change. Participation in the decision-making process of the Community, increased contact with other European civil servants with different traditions of administration, and service in the Community staff might, it was suggested, produce 'a feedback' into the British Civil Service.(5) If there has been movement in these directions it is hard to point to contact with the Community as a significant influence as yet.

Whitehall's impact on the Community's administrative methods and practices has probably been more extensive than the reverse. There had been suggestions that British officials from a profess- ional and respected Civil Service might be able to make a contribution perhaps comparable to, though different from, that of the French to solving some of the inevitable problems of running a multinational organisation, where the difficulty was to develop a coherent management style and tradition amongst so many disparate influences. Sir Christopher Soames had said in 1971 in his lecture commemorating the golden jubilee of the Royal Institute of Public Administration, 'I think it is commonly appreciated in the Communities that British entry will help ... to ensure administrative efficiency', adding 'of course Britain holds no monopoly ... but it is generally recognised that we have a long tradition of combining strong parliamentary government with efficient and effective administration'(6). In the event the first impact of British officials was less than might have been expected. There is no doubt that their credibility was undermined by the renegotiation and the referendum. They were treated politely as people with interesting ideas on administration, but who might be leaving shortly, and so what was the point of taking their views and ideas seriously? The doubt lasted some eighteen months and used up the span of the first enlarged Commission when the broom was newest. Again, the Britons who came did not include as many as had been hoped of the brightest and best from the Civil Service, who would have had more chance of making a greater impact. Perhaps expectations were anyway somewhat misplaced and exaggerated. It would have been difficult and probably undesirable for newcomers to have had an immediate and radical effect. Nevertheless, in the opinion of one well placed observer inter- viewed, it was sad to see the Dutch and Germans (who had hoped for a more significant contribution) disappointed in 1974 and 1975.

This is not to say that the injection of so many Britons has had no effect. Over almost ten years there have been gradual changes as a result of the influence of all the new member state nationals. They had found efficiency and effectiveness impaired by, for example, the formal and hierarchical aspects of the administration, by excessive compartmentalisation and lack of internal communication, and by the weak central management of staff and methods. Their more informal approach, at one level in their use of first names where surnames had been the form, at another in bypassing the time-consuming formal and hierarchical procedures by informal consultative telephone calls, was thought to have improved personal and working relationships. British concepts of teamwork are said to have contributed to an atmosphere where there is now a more widespread informal exchange of views and more open discussion. The increased use of English was inevitable, though in the Council a major impetus was to be the appointment of a Danish Secretary-General who worked in English. French remains the chief working language in the Community. Many of those interviewed felt that increased use of English brought with it a brevity of style and a directness in coming to the point, which was eroding the elegant Cartesian logic of the established French model. There is now, it is said, more likelihood of internal papers reviewing alternatives and anticipating contrary arguments in the style of British administration rather than arguing logically and powerfully as before for a single course of action.

The less than efficient induction of the newcomers itself had demonstrated the necessity of one measure influenced by British civil service precepts, namely, the codification of internal procedures, which had never been done in the pioneering days of the Community. New member state officials in the Secretariat-General had an influence in securing the drawing-up of a manual of procedures which selected and recommended the best of current practice, and which, though never formally approved by the College of Commissioners, did become sufficiently established and used to introduce a measure of harmonisation into the variety of existing traditions.

Other organisational and institutional changes in the Secretariat-General and elsewhere were ascribed in part to British influence. There was the adoption of a more rigorous Treasury O and M-type system of internal inspections, which was aimed at correcting the inappropriate distribution of staff. There were improved methods of physical and paper security and reforms of regulations governing missions and delegations abroad. There were improvements in documentation; the introduction of a system of putting a summary of each proposal into the computer together with its financial implications, and a ten-line summary of each proposal sent to the College of Commissioners. New member state officials joined with some from the old in pressing for greater internal communication and better co-ordination, and were instrumental in getting more internal groups established, ad hoc or permanent, to discuss matters of interest to more than one directorate-general.

In the personnel field, with a British Commissioner for Personnel between 1977 and 1981, and high-ranking Britons in the Personnel Directorate-General, there had been hopes of introducing some techniques on the British civil service model. Some changes were achieved, such as an improved system of confidential reporting and a diminution of the practice of rigged examinations or concours bidons, a formerly much used backdoor method of establishing temporary officials as permanent which shrank before the combined onslaught of the unions and Messrs Jenkins, Tugendhat, and Noel. However, in the personnel field in general, as in others, in the face of the dinosaur-like qualities of the Commission, the effect of proposed reforms has so far been marginal rather than radical, peripheral rather than structural.

One major possible source of change and improvement in the internal organisation and procedures of the Commission was the report much quoted in this study, of the Independent Review Body under Mr Dirk Spierenburg, set up by Roy Jenkins as President, to examine how the Commission's organisation and staff resources could best be adjusted to meet future needs. The initiative was partly the result of pressure for reform from the British and other new member state nationals. Though totally independent, the report's recommendations 'to improve administrative efficiency, career planning and introduce a greater flexibility in the use of staff' and 'to place greater emphasis on management qualities' were directed at areas which had especially concerned them. They had pressed particularly, for example, for job mobility, disliking the way in which people were allowed to specialise to the extent that they stayed in their jobs for as long as twenty years, becoming set in their ways, obstructive of new ideas, and irreplaceable. Spierenburg endorsed the concept, already received wisdom though little practised, and insisted that mobility be necessary for promotion. It remains to be seen, however, if many of the Spierenburg recommendations which reflect the ideas of the newer member states will in the end be put into effect.

Since Britons have been on the staff of the Community institutions, there has been a certain lessening of the distance between Brussels and Whitehall, an increased mutual familiarity and understanding. It could scarcely be otherwise. The institutions are still necessarily cast in a mould which strikes newcomers from the UK as very Continental, very different from those to which they are accustomed, and it will remain that way. Britain is after all only one of ten member states who have cast their ingredients into the pot-pourri of this particular multinational organisation and can indeed claim no monopoly of administrative wisdom. At the same time, the UK authorities have taken useful measures, perhaps belatedly, to ensure that their nationals operate within the Commission and Council on a similar basis to their fellows, and this should contribute to their being better able individually and severally to reach their full potential there.

NOTES

(1) The Sunday Times: 26 June 1977, 'The EEC needs open plan for recruiting staff'.

(2) Question by Mr. Newton Dunn, European Parliament, 7 November 1980, Question no. 112/80 'National officials employed at the Commission'.

(3) See also Lawrence Scheinmann and Werner Feld, 'The EEC and National Civil Servants of Member States', International Organisation, Winter 1972, p.131.

(4) Proposals for Reform of the Commission of the European Communities and its Services. Report by an Independent Review Body under the Chairmanship of Mr Dirk Spierenburg, EEC Publication, 1979, p. 38, para.108.

(5) D. Coombes, Towards a European Civil Service, Chatham House/PEP European Series No.7, 1968, pp.59ff.

(6) Sir Christopher Soames, 'Whitehall into Europe', Public Administration, Autumn 1972, Vol. 50, pp.271-9.

V EPILOGUE

The enduring problem for the UK in Community staffing remains the numerical under-representation in the institutions which originated from the results of the recruitment in 1972-3. The situation which arose in 1982 whereby Britons were temporarily over-represented at the A-1 level was likely to have the effect of diverting attention from the serious extent of the continuing problem in the lower grades, and its implications for the future. This is a problem which is the primary responsibility of the Community institutions as independent organisations, but with which, because of the unique role and functions of the Community in the national affairs of member states, the national authorities are necessarily closely associated. The institutions, under pressure from other member states in a similar position, are alive to the potential difficulty for them of an uneven distribution of nationalities and are concerned to remedy it. The principle of 'harmonious geographical distribution' has been specifically endorsed by member states in the Committee of Permanent Representatives. Yet implementation of the principle remains difficult. The institutions are constrained by conservative attitudes, reinforced by the reluctance of member states to fund additional spending on staff matters, and are unwilling and unable to adopt bold measures. It might be possible to solve the problem at a stroke by holding remedial recruiting competitions in deficit member states to fill additional posts to make up the numbers at all grades; but, important as it is, national imbalance is only one among several priorities. The Germans, for example, argue that efficiency and economy are also priorities and the UK does not dispute this. There is also the effect of any such action on the career prospects and morale of existing staff to be considered. Solutions involving quota systems for recruitment and advancement are resisted as contrary to the spirit of European co-operation and likely to have

89

the effect of reducing the calibre of the staff by restricting the Community's right to recruit the best possible candidates. A moratorium on recruitment from over-represented states would be difficult to implement for political and structural reasons.

Realistically the best hope for amelioration lies in a gradualist approach; in affected member states maintaining sustained pressure on the institutions and working with them to identify and use every opportunity to redress the balance. There has already been some success in forcing the problem to the forefront of their attention such that, while overt discrimination in favour of under-represented states is legally very difficult, actual appointments both on entry and on promotion may be swayed by considerations of 'harmonious geographical distribution'. Candidates 'deemed suitable for employment' from under-represented states may be the first to be offered jobs after general competitions, and internally 'harmonious distribution' may be more widely included as one criterion for promotions. There are ideas and proposals for reform current in Brussels, many of which were advocated in the Spierenburg Report and which could be adapted to alleviate the problem. Early retirement proposals intended to relieve promotion blockages could be aimed primarily at encouraging suitable and willing officials from over-represented states to go. The idea of limiting external A3 appointments to 20 per cent might include a special provision for priority for appointees from the under-represented member states. The proposal to recruit 200 temporary staff at A4-5, intended to foster contacts with national administrations and import expertise, could include provision for suitable persons from the under-represented states to be eligible for permanent appointment. The dilemma is to find legally valid ways to balance the concern of the Community and the member states to achieve a 'harmonious distribution' with their parallel concern to protect the independence of the institutions, and the interests of existing officials, for example, in improving their career structure.

In the particular case of the UK the benefits to be derived in Brussels and Whitehall from roulement and the pattern of employment of British civil servants in the Community - where they are fewer than those from other national administrations, where those who go do not tend to come back, but where temporary assignments are popular - argue for focusing some attention on ways of enabling and encouraging more civil servants to serve in the Community. In view of the Commission's acknowledged need for increased and continuing contacts with national administrations, the UK Government might have success in working with it to achieve an expansion of existing exchange and in-service training schemes with perhaps an added emphasis on the under-represented states. Schemes for a limited number of temporary secondments at all the 'A' grades might have a better chance of implementation if common cause to press for their adoption were to be made with member states such as France, who are not under-represented but are in favour of secondment in principle.

At the same time, however, a high level of interest in and priority for the demands of Community staffing within the Civil Service has to be encouraged and maintained. Establishment Officers must continue to be pressed to draw any opportunities which occur in the institutions to the attention of candidates good enough to be eligible; notices of vacancies at whatever level, A, B or C, in every institution need to be widely and promptly distributed. Though there is competition for the services of clever young Higher Executive Officers and Administrative Trainees, the option of service in the Commission must be kept before them. With restrictions on recruitment above A6 - 7, it is they who are the civil servants most likely to have the opportunity to go to Brussels; they are also likely to be more mobile-minded than their seniors. With the current contraction of the Civil Service and the reduction of promotion opportunities, service in the Community could prove more widely attractive now than heretofore. A wider dissemination of information about how best to go about securing a satisfying and rewarding job in the Commission, and adequate preparation for the differences to be expected in the working environment perhaps through the Civil Service College or a specially prepared booklet, might increase the immediate effectiveness and long-term efficiency of those who do go. Above all, the rate at which the image of life and work in the Commission is changing within the Civil Service needs to be accelerated, and here the activities of the Civil Service College are likely to be helpful. There needs to be a wider recognition that, whatever the known frustrations and inefficiencies generated by the multinational environment, there are jobs to be had there which, as former civil servants can attest, are just as challenging, rewarding, and important as those which Whitehall has to offer, if not more so; and moreover, that it is important that high calibre people be encouraged to seek them.

Though civil servants are in some ways the natural constituency of recruits for the Community, the rights of non-civil servants to have access to the opportunities the Community offers above the most junior grades, few though they may be, must also be accommodated, especially in times of high unemployment. The Commission does occasionally advertise specific posts above the entry levels. At the A1-3 levels, where likely candidates need government backing, notice of vacancies is frequently so short and the posts so uncertain that it is considered impractical to advertise them. The idea put forward(1) that publicity could be given at regular intervals to some central point in Whitehall (in practice the Management and Personnel Office) to which interested parties could write to register a general interest in openings in their field has been considered impractical up to now. If such appointments are to be truly open to all the talents and are not to be regarded, however unjustly, as a civil service preserve, then action on the suggestion and the establishment of such a register would be a desirable innovation.

While recruitment is chiefly confined to the entry level, however, it is clearly important for all the under-represented states to work with the recruiting authorities of the institutions in order to maximise the pass rate of their candidates in an attempt to make up lost ground. Briefing candidates on what they can expect, as the British now do, is an important innovation likely to pay dividends, and it might perhaps be further extended to include pre-course training for candidates, such as the Dutch authorities arrange. It is also open to the deficit member states to try to remove any factors which discriminate, however unintentionally, against their nationals. The Dutch authorities, for example, were recommended by the working party on the subject(2) referred to in Chapter I to bring political pressure to bear to adapt the recruitment and selection procedures to the Dutch situation and background. Some educational and cultural factors present obstacles which are not easily removed. The British candidates, for example, are not likely to be as competent at languages as their continental counterparts, for reasons of geography and schooling. While there may also be a case for entrance examinations tailored to the circumstances of the different member states, it would most likely be rejected as too difficult to administer and too wasteful of resources.

Other problems are more tractable, however, and might repay attention by the authorities. The British Government has already argued a case, for example, for lowering the upper age limit at the A7 entry grade, 32, because Britons graduate younger than their continental counterparts and can be at a disadvantage in competition with the more mature experienced candidates from the Continent whose education in any case prepares them better for the concours. Though the British Government has so far been unsuccessful in this, it might consider returning to the point. Alternatively, the active use of the A8 grade with a lower age limit of, say, 25, might be combined with the existing rules for A7 to make the competition more equal. Again the Commission's ruling that graduates cannot be employed except at the A grade discriminates in effect against British secretaries, because those Britons who have a sufficiently high standard in languages are frequently language graduates. Largely due to British pressure, graduates have recently been allowed into the B grades but not yet into the secretarial grades, and renewed pressure here might produce results. More simply, British candidates have tended to disqualify themselves at the first hurdle, application, when they neglected to include requested documentation of their qualifications, a requirement more usual on the Continent than in Britain. Adjustment on these kinds of matters, establishing a greater degree of flexibility, is an area to which national authorities might usefully address themselves.

Meanwhile there is an urgent need to expand the pool of potential candidates, as a means of helping to maximise the pass rates of Britons. The Commission, and still more the Council, are conscious of not being able to command the kind of regular constituency of interest which Shell and ICI or the Civil Service Commission can attract with their annual recruitment of some 200 graduates. Community institutions recruit a total of 60-70 graduates from all the ten member states together, at intervals of two or three years. Nevertheless, their difficulty can be overstated. The FCO and the Houses of Parliament probably recruit fewer staff per annum but are established goals amongst graduates. There is a strong case for a more vigorous programme of publicity about employment opportunities generally at all grades from A to D within the Community, and perhaps a heightened role here for the London office of the Community. For the A grades there is room for a more intensive and extensive cultivation of contacts in likely institutions of higher education, polytechnics as well as universities, and with appointments boards and careers advisers, so that the possibility of jobs in the institutions between two and five years after graduation is put into the minds of teachers and advisers as well as students at a stage when decisions about careers are being made. The scheme for in-service training for periods of between three and five months (as a stagiaire), which is aimed at young people from the universities and both the public and private sectors, deserves wider publicity, especially as it has proved a well trodden route into permanent service with the Commission (see

93

Appendix VI).

There is a crying need for more published information on life and work within the institutions, written in an attractive and accessible style. Too often recruiting material produced by the Community has been written in off-putting 'Eurospeak' English. What is required is a publication on the lines of the Civil Service Commission booklet outlining careers in the Civil Service. Indeed, it would be a useful innovation to have included in that booklet a note drawing attention to employment opportunities in the European institutions as they are likely to appeal to the same clientele.(3)

It is important for the Community and the UK alike that a high level of interest and concern for the subject of Community staffing continues to be maintained in the government and in Whitehall, and that such an interest is communicated to all the Community institutions. Though the Council Secretariat and the Commission have been the focus of this study, all the institutions, including the European Parliament, suffer a degree of British under-representation. Any, such as the Court of Auditors in Luxembourg, which have a particular need for expertise in areas where Britain's practices differ from those of her partners, should command special attention. Continued close monitoring of the staffing positions, a readiness to recognise and seize opportunities to work with the institutions to help them improve the national balance, together with demonstrable concern to support the legitimate interests of Britons working in those institutions, may help repair the deficiencies of the past. They may go some way to improving the British contribution to the efficient working of Europe, at the workmanlike but vital level of the nuts and bolts. In this as in other aspects of the UK's relations with the Community, most effective of all would be the establishment of a political climate more generally favourable to the Community and Britain's part within it.

NOTES
(1) Sunday Times, 26 June 1977, 'EEC needs open plan for recruiting staff'.
(2) Report from the Working Party on Workshops for potential candidates for A grade competitions at the European Commission: the Dutch ad hoc group on recruitment, 1981, unpublished.
(3) The MPO is now making arrangements to publicise more widely the employment opportunities offered by Community institutions.

APPENDICES

APPENDIX I: The Survey and Questionnaire

a)   The survey
The information on the experience of Britons in Brussels was gathered from interviews conducted between autumn 1980 and autumn 1981 on the basis of a questionnaire (q.v.) with a random selection of 15 per cent of permanent Brussels-based officials who were not in cabinets, at each of the A grades. In the Commission they were selected from a computer list of Britons dated 27 March 1980 and made available by DG IX. Every fifth name within each grade in each Directorate-General or Service, taken in sequence, was selected, except where the person so selected had already been interviewed as background, or was unavailable (for example, because of leave of absence or posting to a Community office abroad), when the next name on the list was selected. This system produced interviewees from every DG in Brussels apart from DG XIV (Fisheries) and DG XVI (Regional Policy) where Britons are numerically and proportionately thin on the ground, and from the Customs Union, the Secretariat General and the Legal Service, but not from the Environment and Consumer Protection Service. A total of 41 Commission officials were interviewed for this survey, one at A1, two at A2, six at A3, nine at A4, eleven at A5, seven at A6, and five at A7. In the Secretariat General of the Council of Ministers, four persons out of the 28 Britons listed in the Situation de l'effectif de la categorie A from the Administration: Bureau des Effectifs, dated 1 November 1980, were selected, one A2, one A3, one A4-5, one A6-7.

All the interviews were conducted on the basis that information, opinions and quotations were non-attributable.

b)   Skeleton questionnaire for interviews with British officials in the Council and Commission of the EEC
1a.   Name
       Age
       Rank
       Rank at joining: date of joining
       DG
       Any previous DG

1b.   Family circumstances
       (e.g. marital status
              spouse in Brussels: spouse's job/pursuits
              children's ages and schools)

96

2a. Educational/professional background

2b. Previous jobs held
(e.g. in international organisations
private enterprise
Civil Service
local government
education
banking and finance)

2c. Last job before joining EC

2d. · Any of these abroad?

3a. How did you come to join the Commission/Council?
(e.g. invited to apply (by whom?)
put name forward in trawl
responded to an advertisement
suggestion of a friend or university teacher)

3b. Did your national government play any role in your recruitment?
What role?

3c. Were there any special factors influencing your interest?
(e.g. European family connections
background in languages
background in Community studies
commitment to the European ideal
directly relevant work experience
desire to work abroad)

3d. What were the decisive factors in your taking the job?
(e.g. salary; nature of the job offered; desire for a change)

4a. Was the job envisaged as:
a) a lifetime career?
b) a stage in a wider career?
c) pragmatically?

4b. Is there a return ticket?
Is it still valid?

5. Were there any problems on first arrival in Brussels
a) Professionally

(e.g.   language
        unsatisfactory job
        work relations
        work methods)
b) Personally
   (e.g. housing
        schooling
        spouse's career
        other family difficulties
        dislike of Brussels)
c) How far were they overcome and by what means?

6.   What do you regard as the chief problem areas now?
     a) professionally
     b) personally

7a. What are the positive features of working for the Comm-
     ission/Council?
     (e.g. job satisfaction
        job interest
        pay
        conditions
        working for Europe
        working relationships
        ability to be effective
        living in Brussels
        lack of opportunity at home)

7b. What are the negative features?
     (e.g. low job satisfaction
        low job interest
        underwork
        overwork
        lack of effectiveness
        work relationships
        lack of job variety
        promotion prospects
        living in Brussels
        other)

8a. Do you consider that your compatriots bring particular
     strengths or weaknesses to the Community's working style?

8b. Have they had a discernible impact on the Community's
     working methods?

(e.g. committee management
language
brevity of submissions
pragmatism of approach
other)

9.   Do you consider that the attitudes and practice of (a) your
national government and (b) highly placed compatriots in the
Commission/Council differ from those of other nationalities
in regard to matters of recruitment and staffing?

10.   Are there any additional comments you would like to make on
any area covered, or any other additional area?

Permanent and Temporary Officials in the Commission - by Nationality
and Grade   31 December 1974

Grade	Germany No.	%	UK No.	%	France No.	%	Italy No.	%	Benelux No.	%	Belgium No.	%
A/1	7	18.4	6	15.8	7	18.4	7	18.4	9	23.6	4	10.5
A/2	23	18.0	21	16.4	25	19.5	22	17.2	27	21.1	13	10.2
A/3	56	17.8	49	15.6	64	20.3	54	17.1	65	20.6	33	10.5
A/4	104	21.1	76	15.4	96	19.5	63	12.8	130	26.4	80	16.2
A/5	86	17.7	72	14.8	74	15.2	100	20.5	113	23.2	67	13.8
A/6	71	24.6	21	7.3	58	20.1	71	24.6	66	22.8	44	15.2
A/7	26	10.8	51	21.2	45	18.7	46	19.1	37	15.4	20	8.3
TOTAL A	373	18.7	296	14.9	369	18.5	363	18.2	447	22.5	261	13.1
B/1	76	21.1	19	5.3	75	20.8	38	10.5	137	38.0	70.	19.4
B/2	74	19.6	3	0.8	79	21.0	57	15.1	160	42.4	98	26.0
B/3	85	22.1	44	11.5	50	13.0	59	15.4	123	32.0	93	24.2
B/4	30	16.9	24	13.5	21	11.8	22	12.4	65	36.5	49	27.5
B/5	5	7.4	10	14.7	10	14.7	15	22.1	16	23.5	8	11.8
TOTAL B	270	19.7	100	7.3	235	17.2	191	14.0	501	36.6	318	23.2
C/1	57	16.3	6	1.7	63	18.1	46	13.2	173	49.6	128	36.7
C/2	143	17.5	7	0.9	121	14.8	94	11.5	450	54.9	344	42.0
C/3	136	12.5	52	4.8	122	11.2	153	14.0	549	50.4	442	40.6
C/4	17	5.9	15	5.2	26	9.0	49	17.0	141	48.8	113	39.1
C/5	3	4.0	7	9.3	6	8.0	21	28.0	25	33.3	17	22.7
TOTAL C	356	13.6	87	3.3	338	12.9	363	13.8	1338	51.0	1044	39.8
D/1	17	9.9	1	0.6	13	7.6	64	37.4	76	44.4	59	34.5
D/2	1	1.1	-	-	6	6.5	50	54.3	35	38.0	29	31.5
D/3	1	1.2	5	6.0	4	4.8	34	40.5	38	45.2	32	38.1
TOTAL D	19	5.5	6	1.7	23	6.6	148	42.7	149	42.9	120	34.6
LA/3	3	25.0	1	8.3	2	16.7	1	8.3	3	25.0	-	-
LA/4	33	25.6	11	8.5	23	17.8	21	16.3	38	29.5	18	14.0
LA/5	51	26.0	21	10.7	27	13.8	35	17.9	52	26.5	27	13.8
LA/6	24	16.9	15	10.6	13	9.2	13	9.2	47	33.1	26	18.3
LA/7	21	8.9	50	21.1	22	9.3	42	17.7	54	22.8	38	16.0
LA/8	10	16.1	8	12.9	5	8.1	9	14.5	19	30.6	9	14.5
TOTAL LA	142	18.3	106	13.6	92	11.8	121	15.6	213	27.4	118	15.2
TOT.GEN	1160	16.3	595	8.4	1057	14.9	1186	16.7	2648	37.3	1861	26.2

Netherlands No.	%	Luxembourg No.	%	Denmark No.	%	Ireland No.	%	Others No.	%	Total
4	10.5	1	2.6	1	2.6	1	2.6	–	–	38
10	7.8	4	3.1	5	3.9	5	3.9	–	–	128
24	7.6	8	2.5	13	4.1	13	4.1	1	0.3	315
33	6.7	17	3.4	12	2.4	10	2.0	2	0.4	493
28	5.7	18	3.7	26	5.3	15	3.1	1	0.2	487
15	5.2	7	2.4	2	0.7	–	–	–	–	289
11	4.6	6	2.5	16	6.6	15	6.2	5	2.1	241
125	6.3	61	3.1	75	3.8	59	3.0	9	0.5	1991
34	9.4	33	9.1	10	2.8	2	0.6	4	1.1	361
37	9.8	25	6.6	–	–	–	–	4	1.1	377
15	3.9	15	3.9	13	3.4	8	2.1	2	0.5	384
12	6.7	4	2.2	11	6.2	4	2.2	1	0.6	178
6	8.8	2	2.9	5	7.4	7	10.3	–	–	68
104	7.6	79	5.8	39	2.9	21	1.5	11	0.8	1368
16	4.6	29	8.3	2	0.6	1	0.3	1	0.3	349
35	4.3	71	8.7	–	–	4	0.5	–	–	819
42	3.9	65	6.0	37	3.4	25	2.3	15	1.4	1089
12	4.2	16	5.5	17	5.9	17	5.9	7	2.4	289
2	2.7	6	8.0	10	13.3	2	2.7	1	1.3	75
107	4.1	187	7.1	66	2.5	49	1.9	24	0.9	2621
3	1.8	14	8.2	–	–	–	–	–	–	171
1	1.1	5	5.4	–	–	–	–	–	–	92
–	–	6	7.1	–	–	–	–	2	2.4	84
4	1.2	25	7.2	–	–	–	–	2	0.6	347
2	16.7	1	8.3	–	–	–	–	2	16.7	12
18	14.0	2	1.6	3	2.3	–	–	–	–	129
25	12.8	–	–	6	3.1	1	0.5	3	1.5	196
20	14.1	1	0.7	24	16.9	1	0.7	5	3.5	142
15	6.3	1	0.4	38	16.0	4	1.7	6	2.5	237
5	8.1	5	8.1	11	17.7	–	–	–	–	62
85	10.9	10	1.3	82	10.5	6	0.8	16	2.1	778
425	6.0	362	5.1	262	3.7	135	1.9	62	0.9	7105

APPENDIX III

Permanent and temporary staff in the Commission – by nationality and grade: 30 June 1980

Grade	Germany	UK	France	Italy	Belgium	Nether-lands	Luxem-bourg	Den-mark	Ireland	Other	Total
A/1	8	7	8	7	5	3	1	2	1	–	42
A/2	24	22	28	24	11	11	6	5	4	–	135
A/3	60	52	57	55	35	26	10	11	2	2	320
A/4	137	78	117	90	102	40	19	4	11	1	599
A/5	85	72.	92	109	57	27	14	18	11	1	492
A/6	69	48	86	77	57	13	8	18	17	3	390
A/7	44	46a	74	34	34a	16	6	11	13	4	282
Total A	427	325	462	396	301	136	64	69	69	11	2260
B/1	87	19	80	60	97	42	29	8	2	6	430
B/2	81	32	91	57	118	30	26	5	2	3	445
B/3	68	33	52	50	111	18	17	12	7	–	368
B/4	28	35	48	48	98	30	18	13	3	2	323
B/5	36	37	34	34	91	23	8	9	9	1	282
Total B	300	156	305	249	515	143	98	47	23	12	1843
C/1	64	6	81	55	185	15	41	3	1	–	451
C/2	146	12	134	156	435	36	78	3	8	3	1011
C/3	69	54	82	109	292	32	56	37	29	15	775
C/4	32	41	25	79	178	12	37	31	13	3	451
C/5	15	32	11	45	91	5	33	21	10	3	266
Total C	326	145	333	444	1181	100	245	95	61	24	2954

APPENDIX III

Permanent and temporary staff in the Commission – by nationality and grade: 30 June 1980

Grade	Germany	UK	France	Italy	Belgium	Nether-lands	Luxem-bourg	Den-mark	Ireland	Other	Total
D/1	9	1	8	83	61	2	9	-	-	-	173
D/2	1	3	3	38	36	-	9	1	-	-	91
D/3	6	6	7	58	50	3	16	-	-	1	147
Total D	16	10	18	179	147	5	34	1	-	1	411
LA/3	3	1	3	2	1	3	1	1	-	2	17
LA/4	49	23	32	30	23	26	2	10	1	1	197
LA/5	50	24	23	39	39	37	2	28	-	9	251
LA/6	24	46	13	37	49	15	1	26	3	4	218
LA/7	57	69	30	74	42	24	3	40	8	23	370
LA/8	2	8	7	9	7	3	1	7	1	10	85
Total LA	185	171	108	191	161	108	10	112	13	49	1108
General Total	1254	807	1226	1459	2305	492	451	324	166	97	8581

a   Including 1 A/8
Source: Commission of the European Community: DG-IX ref. IX-A-2.

APPENDIX IV

Officials of the General Secretariat of the Council of Ministers – by nationality and grade: 16 November 1980

Country	Permanent staff							Temporary staff							Auxiliary staff						General Total	per cent
	A	L/A	B	BST	C	D	Total	A	L/A	B	BST	C	D	Total	L/A	B	BST	C	D	Total		
Belgium	18	23	32	15	186	74	348	1	-	-	-	2	-	3	-	-	-	-	4	4	355	23.82
Denmark	6*	42	1	-	46	-	95*	1	-	-	-	-	-	1	-	-	-	5	-	5	101*	6.77
Germany	33	45	15	6	85	5	189	-	-	-	-	-	-	-	-	-	-	3	-	3	192	12.88
France	31	21	17	7	116	23	215	-	-	-	-	-	-	-	-	-	-	-	-	-	215	14.42
Ireland	7	6	1	-	16	-	30	-	-	-	-	-	1	1	-	-	-	-	-	-	31	2.08
Italy	31	50	10	6	146	84	327	-	-	-	-	-	-	-	-	-	-	3	-	3	330	22.14
Luxembourg	2	2	2	1	6	1	14	-	-	-	-	-	-	-	-	-	-	-	-	-	14	0.93
Netherlands	13	29	9	2	44	1	98	-	1	-	-	-	-	1	-	-	-	-	-	-	99	6.57
UK	28	39	5	-	44	2	118	-	-	-	-	-	-	-	-	-	-	-	-	-	118	7.91
Others	-	1	-	-	4	1	6	-	14	-	-	14	-	28	-	-	-	1	-	1	35	2.34
Total	169*	250	92	37	693	191	1440*	2	15	-	-	16	1	34	-	-	-	12	4	16	1490*	+100

* plus non-established staff.

Source: General Secretariat of the Council of Ministers.

104

APPENDIX V

Results of the 1979 Concours for entry to A6-7 in the Commission at 17 June 1980

	Economic COM/A/143		Legal COM/A/153		General COM/A/154	
	Successful	Appointed	Successful	Appointed	Successful	Appointed
Germany	14	10	18	11	15	7
Belgium	7	3	8	2	8	2
UK	16	12	14	9	17	10
Denmark	5	4	3	3	6	3
France	14	8	17	15	21	15
Ireland	3	2	3	3	6	5
Italy	11	5	16	1	16	7
Luxembourg	-	-	4	3	2	1
Netherlands	3	1	6	5	6	4
Total	73	45	89	52	97	54

Source: Commission of the European Community: DG-IX

Extract from the rules governing in-service training periods with the Commission of the European Communities
(Decision of the Commission of 16 March 1976)

A   Administrative in-service training periods
The Commission organises twice a year in-service training periods lasting from three to five months, for candidates from universities and from the public and private sectors. The training periods start on 16 February and 16 September each year.

Aims and organisation of in-service training
The purpose of in-service training with the Commission of the European Communities is:
- to give trainees a general idea of the objectives and problems of European integration;
- to provide them with practical knowledge of the working of Commission departments;
- to enable them to acquire personal experience by means of the contacts made in the course of their everyday work;
- to enable them to further and put into practice the knowledge they have acquired during their studies or professional careers.

Part of the period may be devoted to preparing a postgraduate thesis or an academic paper, provided that this does not interfere with the training programme.

Admission to in-service training does not confer on trainees the status of officials or other servants of the Communities. It in no way entitles them to be appointed by the Commission.

Admission and selection of university students and public or private sector employees
Trainees are in principle selected from among nationals of the Member States of the European Communities. However, a limited number of nationals of non-member countries may be accepted.

The following may apply:
a) university graduates or holders of diplomas equivalent to university degrees awarded at the end of a full course of study;
b) students who have successfully completed at least four years (eight semesters) of university study;
c) public or private sector employees, provided they have a university degree or equivalent diploma, or have been engaged for at least three years in advisory duties.

For applicants referred to at (c), the Director-General for Personnel and Administration may fix the date of commencement and the length of training periods case by case.

Trainees must be under thirty.

Applicants must have a thorough knowledge of one Community language and a satisfactory knowledge of one other.

Applicants from non-member countries need have a good knowledge of only one Community language.

Applicants are selected on the basis of qualifications; an appropriate geographical distribution will be maintained.

Priority is given to applicants on the basis of the results obtained during their studies. Preference will be given to applicants:
- who have completed or started a course on European integration;
- who hold posts in the private sector or in the public service which require a thorough knowledge of Community activities.

On the basis of these criteria, the Director for Welfare, Training and Staff Information draws up the list of applicants and sends it to the relevant Commission departments for their proposals. Where possible, this list will include the names of at least twice as many applicants as there are training places available.

B In-service training for conference interpreters
Special training periods are organised for trainee interpreters.

Applicants must:
- be university graduates
- have one of the six official Community languages as their mother tongue, and understand perfectly speeches in two other Community languages;
- show that they have the qualities required of conference interpreters.

The purpose of the training is to provide those concerned with the theoretical and practical knowledge required to work as conference interpreters.

The length of these training periods is set by the Director-General for Personnel and Administration. It may not exceed six months. The start of the period is also fixed, case by case, with the Director-General of Personnel and Administration.

C Training grants

A training grant may be awarded to the trainee. The number of grants depends on the availability of funds in the budget.

The grant is now fixed at 16.500 bf per month of training and a monthly supplement of 3,400 bf is given to married trainees whose spouses are not gainfully employed.

Applications must be received $4\frac{1}{2}$ months before the start of the training period and be addressed to:

Commission of the European Communities
Directorate-General of Personnel and Administration
Division Training and In-service Training
200 rue de la Loi
B-1049 Brussels (Belgium)

Commission document 1305/IX/E/78.

Studies in European Politics. This series provides brief and up-to-date analyses of European political issues, including developments in the European Community and in transnational political forces, and also major problems in particular European countries. The series is edited by the Head of the Centre, Dr Roger Morgan. The research is undertaken by the European Centre for Political Studies, established in 1978 at the Policy Studies Institute with the sponsorship of the European Cultural Foundation.

1. David Coombes, The Future of the European Parliament, 1979, pp.136, £3.95.

2. Geoffrey and Pippa Pridham, Towards Transnational Parties in the European Community, 1979, pp.26, £1.80.

3. D. Coombes, L. Condorelli, R. Hrbek, W. Parsons, S. Schüttemeyer, European Integration, Regional Devolution and National Parliaments, 1979, pp.45, £2.25.

4. Carole Webb, Eurocommunism and Foreign Policy, 1979, pp.81, £2.95.

5. G. Bibes, H. Menudier, F. de la Serre and M-C. Smouts, Europe Elects Its Parliament, 1980, pp.69, £2.50.

6. Jay G. Blumler and A.D. Fox, The European Voter: Popular Responses to the First Community Elections, 1982, pp.183, £4.50.

Also, with the Institute for Research in Public Policy, Canada, Regionalism and Supranationalism: Challenges and Alternatives to the Nation-State in Canada and Europe, 1981, pp.129, £4.95.

Books:

Stanley Henig (ed.), Political Parties in the European Community, 1979, Allen and Unwin, pp.314, £10.50 (softback £4.95)

David Coombes and S.A. Walkland (eds.), Parliaments and Economic Affairs, 1980, Heinemann Educational Books, pp.238, £13.00.

David Coombes, Representative Government and Economic Power, 1982, Heinemann Educational Books, pp.208, £12.50, (softback £6.95).

Beate Kohler, Political Forces in Spain, Greece and Portugal, 1982, Butterworths, (German edition, 1981), pp.288, £27.50.

Roger Morgan and Stefano Silvestri (eds.), Moderates and Conservatives in Western Europe: Political Parties, the European Community and the Atlantic Alliance, 1982, (in cooperation with the Istituto Affari Internazionali, Rome), (Italian edition, 1982), Heinemann Educational Books, pp.280, £14.50.

Roger Morgan and Caroline Bray, Berlin and the European Community: the policies of Britain, France and West Germany, forthcoming.

Giles and Lisanne Radice, European Social Democracy in the 1980s: a comparative study in policy developments, forthcoming.

The Working of Coalition Government, (ed.), Vernon Bogdanor, forthcoming.

London-Paris-Bonn: Bilateral relationships in Community and Alliance, (ed.), Roger Morgan, forthcoming.

109